TELL ME WHAT TO DO

by GARY DAHSE

How to Build
a Strategic Plan
For your Life

ISBN-13: 978-1987516777
ISBN-10: 198751677X

TELL ME WHAT TO DO

BY GARY DAHSE

How to Build a Strategic Plan for your Life

DISCOVER

An operating system for your life
with a proven process that works!

A DETAILED ROAD MAP TO:

Financial Security
Emotional Awareness
Spiritual Maturity
&
JOY!

"It makes no difference if you're 17 or 70. You can always learn from your experiences of the past to enhance your future."

"YOUR DESTINY IS SHAPED BY THE QUALITY OF YOUR PERSONAL RELATIONSHIPS." *– Gary Dahse*

"A self-help book without all the Rah-Rah!!
A Proven Operating System for Achievement
for obtaining financial freedom, emotional
awareness and a continuing quest for spiritual
maturity in the shortest amount of time,
with the least amount of brain damage,
regardless of your age, education, background
or circumstances."

Read

&

Enjoy!

To Morgan and Matt -

The finest daughter and son a dad

could ever dream of having.

I am truly the "Proud Father"!

Praying for abundant blessings for you both.

May you each discover your extraordinary passion

and live lives filled with pure

JOY!

TABLE OF CONTENTS

ACKNOWLEDGMENT

Gary Dunkum, what a great friend in Christ and an intellectual Godsend. Without his support and help, this book would have never materialized. Countless numbers of changes, editing and lots of wisdom and input. Thanks for supporting this effort with great vigor, loyalty and friendship. You are very much appreciated! – Gary Dahse

Reflections on "TELL ME WHAT TO DO": Like Dahse, most of us have things in our past we wish hadn't occurred. He is an outstanding motivator and pretty good author. Most of us need motivation – some more often than others. All would benefit greatly from the direction/principles described here. "Meaningful" change requires displacing existing habits. "Wishin & hopin" is not a strategy! I have seen outstanding, real life results of Dahses' mentorship. It would have been GREAT to be a "fly on the wall" during the Pedernales days. "Higher powers" are interesting, but there's only ONE that's "there." Excellent book...IF you're ready for it!

Gary Dunkum
Friend

A FORWARD LOOK

In this book, Gary Dahse has taken cutting edge thought leadership in the field of contemporary moral psychology and created a simple, straightforward "how it works" methodology with immediate added value to human transformation enterprises – cultural, organizational, group and individual. The insightful contents point any reader, who has the courage to engage the journey of self-discovery, beyond themselves to self-actualization solutions. The method has demonstrated cross-cultural utility. Stated simply, his five-stage model from self-awareness to spiritual maturity is clearly aligned with the rich body of successful personal transformation literature.

Dahse shares his success in seeking moral integrity through the application of principled based methods and engaging the body of human and sacred wisdom provided first through ancient scripture and tradition, then through the western enlightenment and scientific revolution, and finally through the current frontier of the neurocognitive social sciences. He has effectively demonstrated an uncanny capability of surfacing 40 years of life's experience by converting his personal lessons learned into a pragmatic life plan roadmap. His personal story of "redemption" will strongly resonate with many readers because it fits the prototype of the American journey in making sense of one's life. He understands the power of story-telling to motivate.

By having the courage to state up front that economic needs are fundamental to living a good life, Dahse is retrieving and taking sides with the British 18th century enlightenment thinkers who set the stage for the ongoing debate on the pros and cons of the human condition. These final declared values were uniquely American at that time. He sides with the "moral psychologists" of that day who shared the belief in the individual's unique ability to make sense of their lives - given a free and just society. He is truly a child of the positive contributions of the American enlightenment.

Dahse's deeper dive into motivation and goal setting explores the long-debated struggle with moral failure – why do good people do bad things? On one hand, he does not complicate his discussion with that citing of the deep and dense literature striving to understand the human complexity of moral failures debated under the topics of egoism, altruism and collectivism. You will not read about the limitations and constraints of teleology, deontology and aretology. You will not read about current debates concerning descriptive and normative approaches to moral comprehension. On the other hand, you will be introduced to the discussion of Goals, Rules and Virtues in simple pragmatic language – a blue collar moral psychological approach that works.

Finally, be assured that Dahse's "novice to expert" character development model has been championed by several distinguished moral psychology academics. This Aristotelian model has stood the test of time. His personality "needs analysis" model has been operationalized, delivered and facilitated transformational success globally*. This is not "pop psychology". Dahse has the gift of communicating highly complex ideas as simple plan forward content. His models and ideas will work for you. May you have a joyful journey…

Frank Reed Larkey PhD.
President, LOCI International

NOTE:

*See the Birkman Method at https://birkman.com/assessment-solutions/birkman-signature-suite/

loci.international.com/white papers/The Beautiful Mind of Roger Birkman

loci.international.com/toolsofthought/The LOCI Relationship 360

See How Emotions are Made: The Secret Life of the Brain by Lisa Feldman Barret

PREFACE

Do you want to get better? It appears to me a lot of people don't! Experience has taught that you cannot realistically ask that question. "Who really doesn't want to get better?" To progress in life, you must want it… really want it! It takes effort and perseverance and a never-give-up attitude. I hear people say they want to lose a few pounds, but they never diet or change their habits. Goals help determine what you want to be, how you see yourself going forward. But you need to develop a plan and a process to make it happen. In TELL ME WHAT TO DO, Gary Dahse takes you through that planning exercise and teaches you a workable process.

Without the traditional, theoretical approach, Dahse provides an experience-based process he has lived and shares what has worked for him. He shares the trials and errors, ups and downs that led him to know that one cannot do it alone. Did he have a God Wink? Maybe, but it wasn't until he focused on Christ and his efforts to forgive and help others that the changes became permanent. Dahse helps you develop a plan to change your thoughts and behavior that will guide you to the results you seek. His focus on the destructive nature of hesitation is key to making lasting change in your life. Baby steps first, and then leaps of faith will propel you and provide the enduring motivation to move on when you have the occasional backslide or when you hesitate to act. Everybody has backslid, so he will focus you on the trend line providing positive feedback to keep going and moving upward.

I have known Gary Dahse since we met at The Exchange Club of the Magic Circle in the Houston Galleria in the late 1960's. We worked on One Nation Under God, Book of Golden Deeds;

serving on the Escape Center Board, major fund-raising efforts and numerous other humanitarian activities. He is a good man driven to excellence. TELL ME WHAT TO DO will provide some entertaining reading and allow you to accomplish whatever goals you set. "Heck, if Dahse did it, so can I."

Ray Jens Daugbjerg KD
Honorary Consul
for Denmark-Emeritus

READER COMMENTS

TELL ME WHAT TO DO is a great book that gives wonderful insight into viewing oneself in a holistic fashion. Gary uses his life's story as a guide showing how you can recover from the pitfalls of life to regain your self-respect and esteem. This is a must-read for anyone who has lost their way and needs a process to put them on the right track. I recommend this book to all who need a great self-help tool.

> Apostle John L. Hickman Jr., Pastor
> The Living Word Faith Center

If one does not have a plan for life—that would equate to getting in a car without a road map and just driving aimlessly around---never arriving at your destination. In this insightful book, Gary Dahse provides a detailed road map to assist the reader in identifying and reaching their financial, relationship and spiritual goals. His past experiences have taken him to the mountain tops and through the valleys of life and now—Gary's new road map takes him toward a life filled with passion, purpose and joy. We all have only one life to live---read this book and learn how to live your best life!

> Dr. Mary Ann Reynolds-Wilkins
> Vice President
> National Commercial Services
> Stewart Title Guaranty Company

An incredible read, but even more important a true road map for success! I was entertained, intrigued, inspired and downright captivated by the message and delivery. Gary Dahse is a master at teaching how to win in business and life, all the while being fulfilled to the maximum. If a seasoned commercial real estate veteran is so inspired, I can only imagine how up-and-comers can cut the curve and achieve unlimited success by learning to set goals and achieve exactly what they want in their lives and careers. I promise you won't put it down once you start!

Susan Gwin Burks
Investment Broker
Senior Vice President
Colliers International

What a helpful guide for living. This little book is filled with lots of "knowledge" for people of every age (including old pros). Golf is a lot like life with its many twists and turns, highs and lows. Gary has produced an excellent guide for anyone wanting to achieve greatness. I encourage you to read, implement and store the information provided in this little jewel. It can change your life!

Doug Sanders
Professional Golfer

I believe the wisdom Gary has gained over his life and shared in this book are spot on. My tenure as an entrepreneurial CEO and coach has led me to wonder why people do such a great job of planning a party or vacation yet do so little with their own lives. I believe success, no matter how you define it, requires goals, a plan and a coach. All high performers have these tools. I also believe we all need the help we can get from credible sources. Gary's words can provide the reader with all those ingredients.

Howard Rambin
Co-Founder,
Moody Rambin Interests

Gary Dahse's new book is an outstanding piece of work that will assist anybody wanting to improve their life. It will also help increase the bottom line for their bank account. Gary has simplified one of the most complex arenas of life and that is how our minds affect everything that we do. He provides a roadmap that teaches a step-by-step proven record to follow to see quick, easy and permanent results. This book is a must read for anyone serious about enhancing their life personally, spiritually and financially. I highly recommend it to anybody who is wanting more from life. Once you start reading this book, it will be difficult to put down. You will find value in every page. Job well done Gary!

Jim Will, Ph.D. Author,
The Power of Self Talk

Fasten your seatbelt. Prepare to be Dahse-ized. This book is a great blueprint for having a better life from someone who has seen and done it all.

Reverend Bill Denham
Pastor, Caring Ministries
St. Luke's United Methodist Church
Houston, Texas

INTRODUCTION

SEX, DRUGS, ROCK-N-ROLL
– NOT!

This book is about a proven technique that teaches you how to build a Strategic Plan for Your Life while you grow toward financial security, emotional awareness and eventually, spiritual maturity. It's about personal mastery focused on the need for a firmly established moral code to chart a path for success. The process outlined applies to everyone, regardless of age, background, culture or experience. It's about a proven process with a road map on how to implement permanent, lasting "Change" in your life and realize all your dreams. This book was written for the common man and for the executive business coach that works with high powered CEO's and leaders. It will help the individual define their personal moral absolutes and help the corporate executives find their corporate moral compass. It's about real-life issues and leadership principals. It's about human beings! It's about a hard-honest look at how we think, act and react.

I firmly believe the process can effect a transformative change in your life, if taken seriously, with an appropriate amount of discipline, denial and creative implementation. Fully understanding the power of "Future Pacing", triggers, imprinting, creative visualization, meditation, repetition and assessment testing are necessary to creating an exceptional "Strategic Plan for Your Life". They are all fully explained in this

19

book, with a road map to show you how to attain your every desire.

You will also be exposed to the unique power of "The Mind-Body Crossover", which will transform your existence into a life filled with discovery and pure, exhilarating joy! It makes no difference if you just graduated from college, just got out of prison, just retired from a long working career, a stay at home mom, a drug addict, an alcoholic, a Fortune 500 CEO or just looking for what to do next. No motivational rah-rah, only a proven process for success and three hidden secrets. Implement the process, practice the secrets and it will change your life. Enjoy the ride.

In addition to "The Mind-Body Crossover" you will also learn about "The Countdown", which is the most powerful way I know to implement immediate change and one of the most compelling reasons why you should learn this technique and read this book. It's especially helpful to individuals battling alcoholism and addiction. You will learn that hesitation is a killer. If you are reading this book, you probably already have the desire to change and some of the knowledge needed to implement change. This book will give you a proven process, a road map and a phenomenal technique that will teach you how to scramble your existing thought processes to ensure you reach new heights in your ability to achieve all your goals. It will teach you how to overcome hesitation and act immediately to change your life forever! I'm hoping it will also be a tool for every global executive coach who teaches leadership and how to implement real meaningful change in organizations. In both cases it's all about connectivity of individuals.

Sex, Drugs, Rock-N-Roll, a pretty true verbal representation, in my opinion, of the cultural revolution, started in the late 1960's. It's also the name of a song written by Ian Dury and Chas Jankel and recorded in 1977. I believe the phrase was a rally cry for the formal inception of the unraveling of the United States as a conservative God-fearing nation. However, I have no interest in pursuing this religious, esoteric, political discussion in this book. Regardless, when "The Revolution" started, I was focused on having what I thought was a lot of fun. It was labeled: Sex, Drugs, Rock-N-Roll. I was a young college kid and didn't have a clue! I went with "The Revolution" – unfortunately. I must have "BUMPED MY HEAD".

I often hear the following statement: "If I'd known then, what I know now, things would be really different" I often wonder, if that statement and its implication would be true in my own case? What about you?

It makes no difference, because my experience tells me, we can't change the past. Wow! You mean I must accept the existing conditions because I created them? What a novel thought. Nope - What a reality! I've come to love and embrace the past, regardless of what has happened in my past, since I can't change it. The big question for me today is: What can I learn from my past to enhance my future, with the remaining time I've got left on this planet to make a difference?

That's what this book is all about. It's about helping all of us, as individuals and corporations to realize the value of our past, and how we can use it to enhance our financial, emotional, mental, physical and spiritual futures. More importantly, I want this book to be a resource for you on how to obtain a tremendous amount of joy in your life by focusing on what really counts and to give you some proven techniques to help you achieve real financial success and unlimited joy, on an ongoing and everlasting basis. It makes no difference if you're 17 or 70, you can always learn from your experiences of the past to enhance your future. It makes no difference if you are 70 years old and financially broke, or if you are worth millions, I have a proven system to share with you in this book, that works. I invite you to implement it in your life, if you are searching for success, significance, purpose and real joy in every area of your life.

When you finish reading this book, you will have a road map to implement a plan that gets real and instantaneous results. Your financial concerns will be eliminated, and your level of joy will increase tenfold. Read and enjoy.

Let's get started with a few questions to help set the tone:

POP QUIZ – TRUE OR FALSE?

- 250,000 people commit suicide in the United States every year. (T) or (F)
- 52% of the people in the world do not have running water. (T) or (F)
- 60,000 kids die every _day_ in the world from lack of clean water. (T) or (F)
- Over 110,000 people die each _day_ from starvation. (T) or (F)
- Over 2.6 _billion_ people in the world do not have basic sewer/sanitation systems. (T) or (F)
- Over 27,500 children die every _day_ from starvation. (T) or (F)

I got these facts from the internet today. All the above statements are true.

If you could afford to buy this book, you are better off than over 97% of the people in the world. Chances are, you are not going hungry today. I mention these facts to help us realize how lucky we are, not having to worry about where our next meal will come from, today. Many people in third world countries, more than you can imagine, don't know when, where, or if their next meal will materialize. I'm concerned about the above facts, and I mention them, so you will get a better understanding of who I am, and what I care about today.

Paul Althoff, a good friend and former co-worker, who does a lot of Christian missionary work overseas, says many of the people he works with in Central America literally do not know if they are going to eat at all when they wake up every morning! The interesting thing he told me was they are the most joyful people he has ever met. They believe that a higher power will provide for them, and they are more thankful and joyous than any of Paul's friends back in the States. What's that all about? I heard these comments from Paul about ten years ago and started a quest to find out what was happening and what I might be missing. Unfortunately, I spent the first 60 years of my existence looking for life in all the wrong places; looking for "happiness" (a term I will define later in this book). Straight out of college, around 1973, I did not care about anybody but me. Me, me, me, me, me! If I'd known then, what I know now, I could have spent a lot more time focused on things that matter. The things that would have brought me more gratefulness, more peace, more joy and certainly more financial freedom. I must have "BUMPED MY HEAD".

I'm the unfortunate victim of an obsessive-compulsive behavior disorder and a recovering addict. Alcohol was my drug of choice, but I have also suffered from several other addictions in my life. I'm a slave to some bad and some good habits. Cigarettes, overeating, whiskey and excessive exercising (marathons), to name a few, are some of the maladies I've overcome because of the process and system I'm sharing with you here. My travels to the Far East, the Middle East, Europe, South America, the U.S. etc. etc. convince me that all people

23

are suffering from some lack of self-worth, self-esteem, self-discovery and a good simple system to help them grow emotionally and spiritually. That's what I'm trying to provide in this book.

This book is intended to help anyone that has a desire to change their life for the better; to provide a system to help you accomplish financial freedom, peace and joy while growing to spiritual maturity. Life is not over until it's over! It's never too late! The Japanese believe life starts over at age 60. Scripturally, in the old testament in the Bible it declares: We are designed to live 120 years. No matter who you are, where you have been, the mistakes you have made, you can always capture or recapture a life filled with passion, purpose and joy. Regardless of your age.

It took me half a lifetime to understand and embrace this major truth. Unfortunately, I had little knowledge, little experience and no wisdom. Today, I finally understand that experience is what bridges the gap between knowledge and wisdom. Back then I had no real sense of reality or a desire to leave a healthy legacy, and I had no experience to lean on. I did not understand or value the concept of going from success to significance to surrender. I was clueless regarding my moral values and had an endless number of character flaws and defects. Moral psychology was an unknown concept to me. I was only focused on success at all cost. Surrender, what's that? When I was fresh out of college, all I could think about was how I was going to make a lot of money and be independent and successful. I was focused on myself (me, me, me, me, me) and determined to succeed at all costs. Nothing was going to stop me. Wrong! If I'd only known then, what I know now.

Gary Dahse

P.S. Setting expectations: At the end of each chapter you will find a Summary and a set of "Golden Nuggets" and "Action Items". Making hand written notes helps "imprinting" and is key to implementation of The Mind-Body Crossover, which is a unique concept explained in this book. I encourage you to take copious notes under the Action Items at the end of each chapter and on every page when necessary. You will understand the immense power of this process when you finish this book.

P.P.S. The key to all great success is action. Taking massive action immediately! Hesitation kills!

P.P.P.S. Let me repeat. When it comes to taking action, hesitation kills! Read and enjoy!

SECTION I
BACKGROUND & DISCOVERY

CHAPTER ONE

IF I'D KNOWN THAT

Financial security, how do we find it in the shortest amount of time, with the least amount of effort? It's a nagging problem for almost everyone, and it hangs around until you solve the problem. Maslow's "Hierarchy of Needs" illustrates a process of needs satisfaction that falls in line with human growth and development, outlined in this book. It starts with self-awareness, then emotional awareness, then emotional maturity, then spiritual awareness and ends with spiritual maturity.

At the bottom of Maslow's Pyramid of Needs, is the basic physiological needs of food, shelter and clothing, which all require either success, money or power to obtain. We must solve this challenge before we move higher up Maslow's Pyramid of Needs satisfaction. Section II of this book is dedicated to helping you solve the success, money, power challenge and provides a proven system to help obtain and satisfy all these needs. You will learn to master The Mind-Body Crossover and The Countdown which will help you overcome hesitation and achieve everything you desire in life. You will learn to embrace, promote and accept change.

But what happens to a person's desires when there is plenty of success, money and power? All at once other "higher" needs emerge and these, rather than physiological hungers, dominate. And when these in turn are satisfied, again new "higher" needs emerge. This is what we mean by saying that the basic human needs are organized into a hierarchy.

The second half of this book, Section III, focuses on the "how to" of acquiring these higher needs on the pyramid. (i.e. safety, love, esteem and finally self-actualization, which is at the top of Maslow's Pyramid). These higher needs require emotional growth, maturity and spiritual growth. It's in the second half of the book where we learn the skills that give us love, peace, joy and serenity, so we can truly enjoy our success, money and power. It's a complete system for living the cycle of life to its' fullest.

Let's get started with a little personal perspective of my journey. I grew up in Weimar, a small town in central Texas, with a population of about 2,000 people. In high school, I considered myself a big fish in a little pond. I was captain of the football team, captain of the tennis team, captain of the track team… and thought I was God's gift to the world! I couldn't wait to get away from my parents and strike out on my own. It was all about me! I was prideful and boastful, and I thought I could make no mistake or do anything wrong! My high school yearbook had a picture of me labeled "The Arrogant Champ". At the time, I thought it was a great compliment. I must have "BUMPED MY HEAD".

I had the greatest mom and dad in the world and virtually grew up in what was a Mayberry RFD situation. (Younger readers will probably have to Google – Andy of Mayberry for a proper explanation of the term – Mayberry RFD). I came from a lower middle-class family, but never lacked the basics. I had a strong Christian upbringing, was taught right from wrong, and pretty much had a great, idyllic childhood in a small Texas town.

Early on, I was warned about grandiose thinking by mom and dad. My parents meant well, but they pretty much told me we were poor, simple people, and I only needed to work hard, get a college degree, believe in God, and not expect too much from life. They emphasized there is no such thing as "get rich quick", and everything good in life comes from hard work, dedication and preparation. Certainly, "don't think you can become highly successful, rich or famous, without hard work!" As a young, aggressive, brash teenager, I ignored a lot of sound advice that caused me a lot of grief as I grew older.

My dad worked for his brother Rubin, who owned the local grocery store in Weimar. My mom was a determined, self-made woman and successful entrepreneur, who owned her own fashion shop and successfully helped start several Lutheran churches in her lifetime. My dad passed away at age 72. My mom lived to 97 and died in 2009. My only sibling, a sister, Susan, and her husband, Don, live nearby in Houston.

I have two beautiful, successful children: My son Matt, is a former investment banker and serial entrepreneur, who operates several businesses from remote locations around the world on his laptop. My daughter, Morgan, is a former actress and a member of TUTS (Theatre Under the Stars). For seven years, as a young talented actress, her accomplishments allowed her to be on stage with Tony Randall and The Osmond Brothers. Today she is using her acting skills in the courtroom as a prosecuting attorney, working for the District Attorney's office.

I've been in the commercial real estate business most of my life. My passion is motivational speaking, mentoring, consulting and training. My speaking career is centered around three unique concepts I call: 1) Future Pacing, 2) The Mind-Body Crossover and 3) The Countdown. Each of these concepts deal with the power of the subconscious mind, and how we control our thoughts to obtain everything we want out of life. More than anything else it teaches us how to take action.

I have a two-pronged focus in my life, as I am living out my dream today as a blessed individual. I spend 50% of my time teaching young people how to discover their "Unique Ability" so they can have great passion for what they attempt in life and be highly successful in all seven (7) areas of their lives. The other 50% of my time is dedicated to helping people in all age categories to live life to its fullest and realize that life starts over whenever I/You, say so! It's all about joy, pure joy! I consider myself a blessed individual today spending my time as a keynote speaker helping individuals live lives full of passion and joy.

It's been a long and interesting journey. I'm just now at the half-way point. Per the Japanese "I continue to arrive". "When the student's ready the teacher will appear." This is one of my favorite quotes. I'm always amazed that I still have much more that needs to be learned and accomplished to reach a fuller spiritual maturity, my ultimate life goal. Learning never stops.

I used to catch myself saying: "If I'd only known that", hoping I could recapture some years, wishing I had caught on sooner. There have been a lot of mistakes and some major regrets that I'm personally responsible for, namely a broken marriage to a great lady. She happens to be the best mother I know, and one of the most talented artists in the country. My two children's successes are a testament to her mothering instincts. My failure to listen and learn, my narcissistic tendencies and addictive behavior made a mess of a 37-year marriage. Regardless of my failures of the past, today I believe I am a better student, willing to listen and learn. Instincts remind me: "When the student's ready, the teacher ALWAYS appears."

Today, I'm fully aware I can't change the past. I know I must have "BUMPED MY HEAD", on numerous occasions in the past. Today I'm not regretting the past, only trying to learn from the mistakes, and be teachable in the future. I'm praying this book helps the teacher show up earlier in your life.

This book features stories that teach some valuable skills for living. When studied and embraced, these stories can help reshape your concepts and beliefs, for what I believe, to be a great blueprint for living life, filled with passion and joy. The process starts with self-discovery, igniting a search for your unique ability. What is unique to you? This book is fashioned around this question. The answer will show you how to have unlimited passion in your life.

Passion is the life blood of this journey we call life.

CHAPTER SUMMARY

GOLDEN NUGGETS:

- "When the student's ready, the teacher will appear".

- The Japanese believe life starts over at 60. It's never too late to start.

- Don't get caught up in grandiose thinking. Think logically!

- Learn from past mistakes and be teachable in the future.

- There is no "get rich quick" formula. Give it up! Now!

- Never stop learning.

- The process starts with self-discovery by igniting a search for your unique ability.

- Passion is the life blood of this journey we call life.

- Hesitation kills!

ACTION ITEMS: (TELL ME WHAT TO DO)

- Start thinking about and looking for your "Unique Ability" today. It will provide passion for what you attempt in life. Write down ten things/characteristics you think are unique to you. (You will be taught the intricacies of this assignment in later chapters).
- Take thirty minutes and write some short notes about what you want your life to look like in the future, (physically, financially, spiritually, mentally, relationally etc.), i.e. what you want to have accomplished in 10 years, 20 years, 30 years etc. This is the starting point for all success. I call it "Future Pacing". Take a mental trip into your perfect future. (You will be taught the intricacies of this powerful assignment in later chapters).

CHAPTER TWO

IS THAT ALL THERE IS?

The years 1971-1976 were a desperately dark period for me. I was in my early twenties. I had it all, and yet, I had nothing! I got out of the University of Texas at Austin and landed a job that eventually led me to become the manager of The Pedernales Country Club, located outside of Austin in the Texas Hill Country. I thought I was living the "good life". The Dream!

As part of my compensation, I had a beautiful three-bedroom luxury condo overlooking Lake Travis, an expensive top-of-the-line company car, unlimited freedom, golfing privileges at all the major country clubs in Austin, and the surrounding neighborhoods, and a decent salary, coming straight out of college in the early seventies. I believe I made $755 a month!! Wow! I thought I was wealthy, when considering the condo and the car! I had attended "The University" in Austin for the previous four years and had "orange" blood running in my veins. An arrogant Longhorn, to say the least. Schultz's Beer Garden, Longhorn football, Texas Fight, Earl Campbell, Hippie Hollow, Darrell Royal, The Orange Bull, Cactus Pryor, The Eyes of Texas, "Hook-em" Horns, kicking ass and taking names, rah, rah, rah, rah, rah! Sex, Drugs, Rock-N-Roll! The race had started! It seemed that nearly everyone at the university smoked marijuana. It was everywhere. It was not uncommon for students to be passing joints to one another on the way to class, and a lot of students attended classes "high" on "weed"!

Johnson, a close friend and former roommate of mine, related a funny story about growing weed in his duplex, out on Red Bluff Road in 1973. Johnson started growing weed in his duplex for self-use and distribution to close friends. Most of his buddies and fellow consumers were growing marijuana under sunlamps in their apartments. This was a common practice for many students. Johnson became an aficionado on growing great weed and eventually started planting the crop in the back yard of his duplex. He had about 100 plants that were growing like weeds, no pun intended. His back yard was partially hidden, surrounded by a wooden fence with a see-through wire entry gate, near the front door on the side of his duplex. The plants were about four-feet-tall and covered the entire back yard. You could only see the crop through the wire gate when entering Johnson's duplex. It was an impressive sight for anyone that loved or consumed marijuana. He was the envy of the UT hippie crowd and many of his fraternity buddies who consumed "weed". One Saturday night, after a UT football game at Memorial Stadium, Johnson hosted a party at his duplex for about fifteen people who came over after the game. He had a great bachelor pad, with a great sound system and three Sony Trinitrons! It was a chick haven and a party house, to say the least, with an unending supply of women, whiskey and marijuana.

We all arrived at the duplex at about the same time after the game and were totally dismayed, i.e. pissed off, to find that the duplex had been broken into and all the TV's and stereo equipment were missing. Having been consuming copious amount of whiskey at the game and smoking weed on the way over to the duplex, everyone was just a little high, drunk and outraged at what had happened to poor Johnson's duplex. We called the cops immediately in hopes of catching these SOB's who ripped off Johnson and his roommate.

While we were waiting on the cops, one of our buddies had a portable stereo system that we brought into the duplex to listen to tunes while we waited. We also had several coolers of beer in the car that we unloaded in the refrigerator, waiting until the police arrived. We were pissed, really - PISSED! Being in an inebriated condition, it took us about five minutes before someone, a "brilliant person" no doubt, realized that we had just called the cops and the back yard was full of WEED!!! When we realized what we had done, we went into panic mode! We theorized that the cops would be arriving any minute, and there was no way they would not recognize the "crop" out back. We were in El Toro Poo, Poo, another name for "deep shit"! In those days, you could easily go to prison for possession of even an ounce of marijuana, much less 100 full grown plants! Yikes!!! It was an absolute hilarious event, watching eight girls and six guys ripping up 100 four-foot-tall, marijuana plants in about 30.3 seconds flat. They finished hiding the plants under a huge tarpaulin in about 1.3 seconds before the cops arrived. It was truly a Laurel and Hardy event! I wish I had a video. Unbelievable!

P.S. I'm not sure, but I think, I might have been Johnson's roommate that year!

It was also a time of football arrogance in Austin at "The University". I believe I attended the University of Texas four years and never saw or heard of Texas losing a football game. Darrell Royal, the UT football coach, was considered by many as the smartest and best football coach in the country. Royal was the first major-college coach to hire a "brain coach", who was responsible for academic counseling in intercollegiate athletics. He was very innovative. I was a benefactor of this innovation when he hired Lan Hewlett to fill this position as brain coach. As a kid growing up in Lockhart, Texas our next-door neighbor was a science teacher by the name of Lan Hewlett. What a stroke of luck for me. Lan's number one job was to ensure that student athletes attended class, got good grades and eventually graduated. When I moved to Austin to attend UT, Lan Hewlett was the first person I sought out. Luckily, he remembered me as the kid next door in Lockhart and helped me get into a lot of choice classes at the university through his knowledge of the professors and class availability. He also introduced me to Darrell Royal one day in his office. I was an arrogant little twit, when telling my friends that I "knew" Darrell Royal! Rah, Rah, Rah, Rah, Rah!

I believe at the time I attended The University; Texas' football record was something like 49-2. As mentioned earlier, I do not recall ever seeing or hearing of Texas losing a football game, in the four years I attended The University! We thought we were the "Kings" of everything. Little did I know that I was starting a journey, a tough, hard journey, of extremely hard knocks that made it quite evident, that I was not the King of anything, much less everything.

God was getting ready to apply some very extreme pressure on top of my stubborn head! For the next 40 years, he taught me some very valuable lessons about two words that I needed to incorporate into my vocabulary. Both happened to start with the letter "D". Denial and discipline.

I was living life in a very fast lane, a fast and furious lane! Smoking one and half to two packs of cigarettes a day, eating unlimited gourmet food from the Country Club restaurants and I had access to unlimited alcohol from three fully stocked bars at the club and in my condo. (The dangerous start of a deadly addiction). I was a space cadet and totally out of control! I was working 12-hour days, seven days a week and partying every night. I was 50 pounds overweight and clueless!

Sex, Drugs, Rock-N-Roll were the norm of the day in Austin in the early 70's. My college buddies, guys and gals, practically lived at my condo out on Lake Travis because of the constant party atmosphere, free booze, free grass and unlimited vices you can only imagine. Nothing was too much. Our drug of choice was MORE!

Austin was a haven for marijuana and the so called "Cultural Revolution" of the sixties and seventies, and almost everyone was partaking in the so called "Revolution". I was no different and used the excuse that "everyone is doing it". I must have "BUMPED MY HEAD".

During my tenure at The University, I ran with a fast group of guys and gals who were constantly on the prowl for fun and more fun. It was a constant party and we were creative about living in the fast lane and thinking of unique ways to make more money to fuel the constant party machine. One of my buddies, Buster and his close friend Kenny, were the creative geniuses of the group. We all played a lot of poker in our spare time at college. Buster and Kenny decided to take our pastime to a higher level by hosting casino parties for profit. The key to success was being able to fill a large room with a lot of people. To do that, it was always helpful if you could get a campus celebrity or two, to attend your party to attract other participants. James Street, the famous longhorn quarterback, and orchestrator of the wishbone offense, was a campus icon. Buster and Kenny came up with brilliant idea of making bumper stickers that read: "Street for President". This bumper sticker garnered a lot of attention and a story was published in the UT student newspaper - The Daily Texan. Street got a lot of publicity out this creative bit of merchandising and was always willing to show up at Buster's and Kenny's parties, making these two guys a lot of dough! Always thinking!

It was also the new age of "Progressive Country Music", which was temporarily replacing Rock-N-Roll, but everything else was the same, including all the other debaucheries of a carnal society to include "free" love. Thank God AIDS had not surfaced yet, as I'm certain half of the college students in the U.S. would have died due to overindulgence. On weekends, the favorite pastime for fraternities on the liberal Texas Campus was a contest called Sport F-ing. You can only imagine how they kept score! Pat K. and Dan B. always claimed to be the winners, but rumor has it they were all talk and no show!

It was crazy! Willie Nelson had just moved permanently to Austin from Nashville and was the leader of the Progressive Country "Outlaw" movement and spent a lot of his free time hanging out at the Pedernales Country Club, and eventually buying it. It was all about "Willie and The Boys!" He and a lot of his buddies, including Waylon Jennings, Jerry Jeff Walker, Charlie Pride, Steve Fromholz, Rusty Weir, Kris Kristofferson and some members of their entourages hung out in Austin, from time to time, to get away from the fans and relax. Willie was quickly becoming an icon after recording his big hit album, "Red Headed Stranger" and his announced permanent move to Austin was the talk of the town and the country. His annual 4th of July Picnic in the Texas Hill Country was all the rage. It became a mini Woodstock, held every year and attended by music lovers far and wide.

I saw Willie for the first time in the pro shop at The Pedernales Country Club one lazy afternoon around 4:00 pm. He was very quiet, shy, unassuming, very kind and humble. I was familiar with who he was, but his "household fame" was certainly not what it is today. At the time, I was the assistant manager of the country club, working directly for one of the owners/managers, Ted Peyton. Ted put me in charge of making sure Willie and his friends were well taken care of when they visited the club. What an exciting job for a guy straight out of college. Sex, Drugs, Rock-N-Roll---Whiskey and MORE!

I had a lot of opportunity to meet some interesting people during my time in Austin and had a lot of funny and interesting stories along the way. I will share some of these with you later, as many hold interesting truths about life, in addition to being funny, interesting and educational. They will teach you about human emotion and human drive and the psychology of winning. Stay tuned.

An interesting story unfolded one afternoon when Ted Peyton and his college roommate, Carroll Overton, played a round of golf at the club with an up-and-coming college prospect named Ben Crenshaw. Ben was already relatively famous, as one of the top college golfers in the country but certainly not as famous as today. It was interesting to watch the competitive nature of these three guys as their desire to win, and enthusiasm for the game was on a completely different level from amateurs. Their competitive obsession and desire to win was displayed during a round of golf one quiet afternoon at The Pedernales. Peyton and Overton were both very good golfers and Peyton was one of the best golfers I ever witnessed firsthand. He went to pro school with Jack Nicklaus and was very competitive, but also very composed and emotionally very mature. He was always aware of his ego and kept it in check. A character trait that I always admired in Ted Peyton. He had a very high emotional quotient, something I will talk about later in this book.

Peyton's golf game was on "fire" this day, and every shot was almost dead perfect. He was four under par after four holes and potentially on track to set a course record at The Pedernales Country Club. Overton and Crenshaw could not believe some of the shots Peyton was making that afternoon on the golf course. On the fifth hole, after birding the first four, something rather unusual happened that made an impression on me about extraordinary confidence, creative visualization, emotional maturity and class. Peyton, has the honors, on the fifth hole, and continues to shoot "lights out", knocking his ball within four feet of the hole for another sure birdie that would put him five under, for the first five holes. This was something no one had ever accomplished on The Pedernales golf course, not to mention the possibility of birding all nine! The fifth hole at the nine-hole Pedernales is located next to the club house and considered "the turn" hole, before you cross the street and continue to finish the remaining four on the other side of the clubhouse. Peyton is standing over his relatively straight and easy four-foot putt for birdie, when his secretary sees him from the clubhouse office and runs out to tell him he has an important call he needs to take. Peyton apologizes to Ben and Carroll and tells them he must take this call and proceeds to calmly pick up his ball and walk off the green! Crenshaw and Overton look on in disbelief and I believe it was Crenshaw who supposedly mumbles something to the effect, that "Mr. Peyton must have lost his mind! No phone call could be that important!"

I was observing this event from the practice putting green next to the clubhouse and adjacent to the fifth hole. I heard the entire story from Overton later that day. I really could not believe what I heard, and later ask Peyton how he could walk away from a potential course record. He proceeded to tell me that "second chances" were free. "All you need to do is take them!" An interesting thought that I had never considered before. He then proceeded to tell me he had visualized a five under score after five holes on numerous occasions and had already accomplished this feat several times, while playing alone in the late afternoons during his practice rounds. He felt confident he would eventually accomplish the task again with witnesses and did not feel the need to prove it to anybody other than himself. If he knew within himself that he could do it, he was totally satisfied. He professed visualization as the key to anyone's greatness! What a lesson on controlling your ego and your emotions. It taught me a lot about self-control and the power of visualization. Thanks, Ted.

The saga at The Pedernales continued. Party! Party! Party! was the norm. Most afternoons I was responsible for entertaining club members and the recording artists ("The Stars") on the golf course for a late round of golf with lots of libations. I can remember heading out to the number one tee around 5:30 or 6 p.m. for nine holes of golf with two or three foursomes most afternoons. It was always a loud, rowdy bunch, with plenty of ego to say the least. The late afternoon tradition called for providing two or three large beer pitchers filled with ice and a quart of Wild Turkey poured on top of each container. These large pitchers were passed between the participants and used as a "communal cocktail glass". Golf carts in those days had small swinging wire baskets attached to the dash to hold drinks and prevent them from spilling. They had large overstuffed seats that were rounded on the top and it was impossible to set a drink on the seat without it overturning when you got out to hit your golf ball. I remember one of our biggest problems was spilling full pitchers of Wild Turkey because the glass pitchers would not fit in the small wire basket cup holders. What a dilemma! One of the "Stars" insisted I solve this nagging problem by fabricating some larger wire baskets to hold the full pitchers of whiskey! Nothing was too much for The Stars!

As mentioned previously, The Pedernales Country Club had only nine holes of golf. The first five holes were on one side of the clubhouse and the remaining four holes on the other side. During these outings, the first five holes were crazy entertainment, as consumption was up, and ball striking was down ---- way down! I don't recall the group ever playing the remaining four holes after the "turn", as consumption had overtaken golf as a priority. Most of the players probably could not see the golf ball, much less hit it!

On several occasions, some of the recording artists would return to the cart barn after golf and play music into the wee hours of the morning, enjoying each other's company and making up songs as they went along. If I would have only had a video recorder. It was classical!

"Liar's poker" was also a favorite pastime of club members and "The Stars". I remember numerous occasions where traditional club members and recording artists would meet in the bar after a round of golf and play "liar's poker". As the evening wore on and the atmosphere became more and more festive, participants would insist on upping the ante. Eventually everyone was playing with larger bills. Occasionally hundred-dollar bills were the norm and you could win or lose a considerable amount of money. I recall one evening, where the libations were considerably out of control and the participants began tearing up larger bills and throwing them up in the air for "Ego-Sake". At the end of the night Ted Peyton would gather up the pieces of these bills and we would tape them together and attempt to return them to the participants the following day. Some nights there were over 15 or 20 larger bills reconstructed with scotch tape. The participants always refused to accept the bills the following morning and telling Ted to: "Just keep-m". Crazy!

The Armadillo World Headquarters in South Austin was the place to hang out and see and be seen. All the up-and-coming progressive country music recording artists would hang out at The Armadillo for impromptu jam sessions, and it was not uncommon to have three or four major artists show up unannounced in one afternoon to jam. I hung out with many of these recording artists who eventually became famous, if they weren't already common household names in much of the country. These guys and gals were a lot of fun, and I felt privileged to hang out with them in the afternoons, playing golf and partying at the Club to the wee hours of the morning. They were living life to its fullest and seemed to have it all.

I made it a priority to spend as much time as possible with these people and their groupies making every effort to keep up with their late-night indulgences and extravagant life styles. The only problem was, I had to get up for work every morning at 5:45 a.m. to organize the country club staff, and they got to sleep-in until 2:00 in the afternoon after a late night of Rah-Rah.

Willie eventually bought the country club from my employer and eventually turned it into a recording studio after I moved to Houston. During his tenure, rumor had it that Willie had some problems with the IRS and the country club was confiscated for back taxes. Legend has it that Willie's good buddy Darrell Royal, football coach of the Texas Longhorns, helped buy back the club and returned it to Willie as a gift! Fact or fiction? I'm not sure.

After several years of this constant party, I was toast! I was burning it at both ends. I can remember waking up most mornings, after about three or four hours of sleep, so hung over that I used to joke I felt so bad my "teeth itched"! It became my famous moniker and my claim to shameful fame. What a sad, saying to have to claim. So, hung over that my teeth itched! I must have "BUMPED MY HEAD".

After about two years of this wild and crazy, uncontrolled lifestyle, I was figuratively in the gutter, and almost literally there as well. I was looking for "something" and was totally befuddled why I wasn't having more fun and enjoying this MORE!!?? Wasn't this "HAPPINESS"? Sex, Drugs, Rock-N-Roll? ---Whiskey and MORE? Not to mention copious amount of weed. I thought I had everything, and most of my friends seemed to be envious of my lifestyle. So, what was wrong? Why wasn't I enjoying this more? I kept asking myself – "Is that all there is?" "Is that all there is?"

CHAPTER SUMMARY

 ## GOLDEN NUGGETS:

- Sex, Drug, Rock-N-Roll might not be all it's cracked up to be. Be careful of constantly altering your physical state with drugs and alcohol. Very dangerous territory.

- Second chances are free. --- "All you need to do is take them!"

- Emotional maturity can help keep your ego in check. This is a good thing.

- "Our drug of choice was MORE!" – Not a good thing. You need the Two D's – Discipline and Denial to bring personal self-control into your life, if you want to be highly successful and totally fulfilled.

- Hanging out with famous people won't necessarily make you famous.

- Hesitation kills!

ACTION ITEMS: (TELL ME WHAT TO DO)

- Make a list of all the dangerous activities you are participating in that could cause you trouble in the future. -------- Be honest!
- List the last five times your ego was out of control in the last month.
- Write down your definition of happiness.
- Write down your definition of joy.

CHAPTER THREE

"WHEN THE STUDENT'S READY, THE TEACHER WILL APPEAR"

I was a narcissist of the highest degree. Later in life, one of my many "shrinks" would inform me that self-indulgence (narcissism) was my most prevalent character defect. I also suffered from clinically diagnosed attention deficit disorder and an overly addictive behavior and lifestyle. What a sad and lowly state! What went wrong? Wasn't this "HAPPINESS"? I had to get out! I was slowly dying… I had to change! But how?

I was determined to change but hadn't a clue how to get started. One day in 1972, I heard that a highly recognized motivational speaker and trainer was coming to Austin. I decided to attend, in hopes of learning something new to help change my life. It was an eventful, eye opening presentation that started me on a quest, eventually leading to the formation of "The Mind-Body Crossover", "Future Pacing" and "The Countdown" that I am sharing with you here. The speaker touted a secret way to accomplish anything you desired out of life by using his proprietary goal setting technique. He also talked about a great book, "Think and Grow Rich" by Napoleon Hill, written in 1937 and recognized as one of the first modern day self-help books. He encouraged us to read this book, as it utilized a technique of "Conceive, Believe and Achieve". In the late seventies, there were a limited number of good self-help books. Nothing like today, where you can buy thousands of self-help books on any subject. I was driven to change this shortage of good material with a process providing a road map for success that really worked, if properly implemented.

The speaker kept repeating Conceive, Believe and Achieve. Today this statement, this mantra, is considered an old paradigm, but at the time got me to thinking about the simplicity of his method. A lot of wisdom in simplicity... "Anything you can conceive and believe, you can achieve." It was considered new age, creative visualization thinking. The entire forty-five-minute speech that night was centered around this statement but didn't appear to give you a plan or process on how to implement a working strategy. (i.e. No road map to success). I spent the next several years perfecting a system, to implement a new concept for achievement. I eventually became well known on the keynote speaking circuit for this system, which I'm sharing with you in this book.

My journey for a new life had begun after hearing this motivational presentation. I was thinking about my future! What was I going to do? Who was I going to become? How was I going to change? The party scene was wearing me out. It was slowly killing me! Booze and marijuana already had an addictive grip on me, and I sensed it. Nope, I knew it for a fact!

I finally hit a wall in 1972, with an eye-opening, life changing experience. The historic Driskill Hotel in downtown Austin was a favorite hangout and watering hole of mine. I would party with friends, college buddies and members of the country club night after night at this famous watering hole. One evening, after copious amounts of partying at the hotel, I decided to go home early to get some much-needed sleep. Tired and run down, I slipped out to my car and started the 45-minute drive back to the Pedernales Country Club on highway 71 West on Lake Travis in the Texas Hill Country. I pulled out on Congress Avenue at about 11:15 p.m., waiting for a red light to change. Impatient and sleepy, I made a life changing decision. After sitting at the red light for what seemed like 3-4 minutes, I decided to roll through the intersection and head home. I looked left and then right, to ensure there were no cops around. The street was totally deserted. Unfortunately, or maybe fortunately, I failed to look in my rear-view mirror as I rolled through the intersection. Blinding lights and a booming siren – YIKES! There was a cop sitting right behind me! I must have "BUMPED MY HEAD".

Sitting at my condo several nights after the Driskill incident, I was convinced more than ever that I needed to change. No, I had to change. Getting thrown in jail for drinking and driving was the lowest point of my life and the last time I visited a jail as a bad guy. I knew in my heart of hearts that I had to change. How stupid and irresponsible could I be?

One night at my condo in 1972, after the Driskill Hotel incident and subsequent visit to the jailhouse, I was watching the Olympics on TV and saw Frank Shorter win the gold medal in the marathon in Munich, Germany. I can remember briefly thinking, sarcastically to myself, about the mantra of Conceive, Believe and Achieve, wondering if I could use his mantra to run a marathon? Wow, what a mind-blowing thought! Being a long-distance runner and miler in high school, I had some idea about long distance running, but 26.2 miles was almost unfathomable! I had never run more than three miles continuously in my life. Was I crazy? Had I "BUMPED MY HEAD"?

I spent several years thinking about the mantra. After considerable study and contemplation, I decided to give the concept a try after watching Frank Shorter win the Silver Metal in the marathon, four years later, in the 1976 Olympics. In 1975, I had moved from Austin to Houston, Texas to change my surroundings, create a new life style, and get a new set of healthy friends. My major goal at the time was to run a full marathon, 26.2 miles.

My concept made a mega leap in 1978, when I read a book called Creative Visualization by Shakti Gawain, a best seller that changed the way a lot of people thought about goal setting and achievement. Shakti had taken achievement to a whole different level, becoming the new "Bible" for self-improvement. Forty years ago, when this book was written there was limited science behind the theory of creative visualization. Today there is overwhelming scientific evidence that we are not mere victims of our biology or circumstances. We now know, how we think and react to the events and circumstances of life, and how they can have a major impact on our mental and physical health. We now know our brains have the capacity to recover from major damage and trauma and we can change the physical nature of our brains by what we think. (i.e. thoughts become things!).

It took a few years and a few false starts, but I finally decided to stop smoking, stop drinking alcohol and stop overeating. All at once! I was going to give it a try. At the time, I weighed 235 pounds, 75 pounds heavier than when I ran my last mile in high school competition. I must have "BUMPED MY HEAD", again.

I can remember the day I discovered Memorial Park, inside Loop 610 on Memorial Drive, in Houston. There was a three-mile trail around an eighteen-hole golf course that became my second home for the next fifteen years. My obsessive-compulsive behavior got the better of me, and I started running every day. I was totally consumed with running and would take time away from my day job to ensure I could get in at least ten miles a day on the Memorial Park track. The "Living K", (Kevin) a close friend of mine and running partner, I met while running my first marathon, would meet me at the park every day for a ten-mile run. We got in 70 miles a week. We ran five, 10-mile runs a week, and a 20-mile run every Saturday. We took Sundays off to rest and recuperate. We continued this pace for the next fifteen years. Unfortunately, I was still consuming copious amounts of alcohol after every days' run, in addition to consuming a lot of chocolate chip cookies and Blue Bell Ice Cream at Bubba's hamburger joint near the park most afternoons. As always, it was all about MORE!

Kevin and I were obsessed with breaking the three-hour marathon, so we could qualify for The Boston Marathon. We trained like maniacs. I got close to the mark in 1978 at the Galveston Marathon. Unfortunately, a hurricane was approaching, and we had to run half the course into 60-70 mile an hour head winds. It was brutal! Kevin ran a 2:57 and I ran a 3:04, my best effort. The only reason I could accomplish this feat, was due to my obsessive-compulsive nature. Not necessarily a good thing! I can remember one 26 mile run in Louisiana, where Kevin and I ran the Crowley Marathon. They ran out of water on the course after about twelve miles. Kevin, being of sound mind and body, stopped when they ran out of water, but not me! My obsessive condition forced me to finish the course, water or no water. I must have "BUMPED MY HEAD". The lack of hydration caused me to urinate blood for the next twenty-four hours. Not a good choice!

I eventually started taking medication for my obsessive-compulsive condition, and my life became a little more manageable and stable even though I continued to abuse my body by drinking alcohol.

During this period of transformation, I had been voraciously reading every self-help book on the market starting to formulate a systematic goal setting approach for achievement utilizing creative visualization and repetition. I spent considerable hours reading philosophy books by Hobbs, Hume, Nietzsche, Descartes and others.

I spent a lot of time creating what I came to identify as the "Mind-Body Crossover". This basic premise of learning how our subconscious mind can turn a thought (from our Mind/Spirit) into a physical reality (Body/Physical). An example is when an architect conceives a picture of a building in his mind, makes a physical drawing on paper, hires a contractor and it eventually becomes a real, physical building. That's called bridging or crossing over the mind-body barrier. A spiritual thought, something you cannot see, turns into a physical structure/reality, something you can touch and see. Where in the brain does this takes place? No one has ever been able to identify where this crossover takes place.

My experience gained from knowledge of creative visualization, the subconscious mind, combined with philosophical thought helped me codify The Mind-Body Crossover. This technique focuses on the need for repetition to create new habits. The only way to break a habit is by substituting a new habit in place of an old one. Whenever you break an old habit, a vacuum is formed in our consciousness which demands to be filled. It must be filled with a new habit or the old one will eventually return. Doing something over and over, again and again, is the only way to break an old habit and one of the best ways to start a new one. Lots of research states that it takes about sixty-six days of repetition to break an old habit or start a new one. This is no easy task and it comes in three phases. The first twenty-two days of trying to form a new habit are very difficult. The next twenty-two are easier and the last twenty-two days can be exhilarating, once you start to see the benefits of the new action. Building a strategic plan for your life requires a lot of new habit formation. Get ready.

My subconscious mind must have been working overtime, training me to think big thoughts. I stopped smoking, stopped drinking alcohol, lost seventy pounds in eight months and ran my first marathon in Houston in three hours and twenty-six minutes in 1976. All a result of mastering the power of The Mind-Body Crossover, Future Pacing and The Countdown.

What was going on? This experience helped me formulate two little known secrets about successful goal setting that I would like to share…that will change your life. They are very powerful, yet simple to implement. I used these two secrets to drop my marathon time down to 3 hours and four minutes within several years and attempted to run an ultra-marathon, 52.4 miles, in 1983. I was totally amazed at the power of these two secrets.

My ultra-marathon attempt ended after running 38 miles due to boredom, not lack of training or physical ability. I was in excellent shape at the time and had several friends run 8-10 mile stretches with me to help keep me enthused. After running for about five and half hours and no other support team members to keep me engaged, I decided to go to the house in a moment of boredom. I regret that I didn't finish, but my level of self-confidence was twice as high, due to the discovery of these two powerful secrets that eventually helped me accomplish beneficial and worthwhile things in my life.

During this transformation I came to realize: Thoughts become things! What an interesting concept. If I think positive thoughts, positive things occur. If I think negative thoughts, negative things occur. Watch what you think! People that are always positive and upbeat create like things. People that are always negative and critical create like things. Choose your attitude carefully and monitor it moment by moment as your subconscious cannot distinguish between real and imaginary. To make meaningful change and eliminate old habits, we must scramble our rote thinking process, to fill the void with new, healthy habits. We will fully explore this scrambling concept later as it holds one of the key secrets to lasting change, a prerequisite for success.

CHAPTER SUMMARY

 GOLDEN NUGGETS:

- "Anything you can conceive and believe, you can achieve."

- You can get anything in life you desire once you master the power of The Mind-Body Crossover, Future Pacing and The Countdown.

- The Mind-Body Crossover. The basic premise of learning how our subconscious mind can turn a thought (Mind/Spirit) into a physical reality (Body/Physical). A secret to powerful goal setting and achievement.

- This Technique focused on the need for repetition to help create new habits.

- To make meaningful change and eliminate old habits, we must scramble our rote thinking process, in addition to filling the void with new healthy habits.

- Lots of research states that it takes about sixty-six days of repetition to break an old habit or to start a new one.

- Future Pacing. The ability to visualize what you want your future life to look like (i.e. be) when you arrive at a future date.

- Thoughts become things!

- Choose your attitude carefully and monitor it moment by moment as your subconscious cannot distinguish between real and imaginary.

- Whenever you break an old habit a vacuum is formed in our consciousness which demands to be filled. It must be filled with a new habit or the old one will eventually return.

- Building a strategic plan for your life requires a lot of new habit formation.

- My level of self-confidence became twice as high with the discovery of these two powerful secrets, eventually helping me accomplish many extraordinary things in life.

- Hesitation kills!

ACTION ITEMS: (TELL ME WHAT TO DO)

- I was thinking about my future! 1.) What was I going to do? 2.) Who was I going to become? 3.) How was I going to change? - Write down your preferred answer to these three questions in the margin of this page. A great "Future Pacing" exercise for your subconscious mind.

- Conceive, Believe and Achieve – If you came to believe in this mantra as a fact, what personal dream would you want to materialize into reality. Write it down in the margin of this page. Think big possibilities.

SECTION II

SOLVING THE SUCCESS, MONEY, POWER CHALLENGE

CHAPTER FOUR

CREATIVE VISUALIZATION & THE MIND-BODY CROSSOVER

Solving the success, money, power challenge, requires a new way of thinking. "Creative visualization is the technique of using your imagination to create what you want in your life." - Shakti Gawain. When I read this definition in the late seventies, I was totally enthralled with the wisdom in the statement. It started me on a path to spiritual maturity that has changed my entire life. It gave me a new way of thinking and looking at Life, God and Purpose. Today, I practice creative visualization every morning when I wake, during my quiet time when I'm still in my alpha/relaxed state. This concept is a vital component of building a strategic plan for your life. Once you fully understand how your subconscious mind works, you can make mega leaps in your quest for living a life full of purpose, passion, joy, serenity and peace, while expanding your self-awareness. I call this having an intentional relationship with your brain. It is a great starting point for fully understanding the concept of Conceive, Believe and Achieve, a vital part of The Mind-Body Crossover.

The Mind-Body Crossover is a term coined to help explain a system I've created to help individuals acquire superior goal achievement. It's a simplified explanation of how we operate between states and the phenomenal power gained once we understand what's happening when we crossover from one state to the next - mental to the physical, spiritual to carnal, subconscious to conscious. Asleep/awake. Dreams/reality.

When and what happens when we crossover from one state to the other? How is a mental thought converted to a physical reality and vice versa? What is the secret to bridging this mind body gap? Is it possible to control and create realities once we are aware of how the system works? The answer is yes. I will be showing you how to create your own realities by harnessing The Mind-Body Crossover, Future Pacing, The Countdown, triggers, imprinting, creative visualization, mind control, repetition, meditation, mantras and goal statements.

As noted, Maslow's Hierarchy of Needs helps codify knowledge of how our brains work and what happens to our state(s) as we move up the Maslow Pyramid of Needs. At the bottom of Maslow's Pyramid is the need for food, shelter and clothing. These are all physical needs. At the top of the pyramid is self-actualization. This is a mental state.

One well known example of operationalizing the "needs" concept is the Birkman Method. Roger Birkman based his social comprehension model of personality on uncovering hidden needs, also described as social expectations. This assessment evokes the unconscious social expectation of how one individual expects "most people" to act. The assessment adds value to personal exploration of unique ability by surfacing the "blind spots" in our social cognition. Its utility has been validated by its great popularity with major organizations, executive coaching, training departments and team building within diverse cultures. Assessment testing is critical for emotional growth.

Food, shelter and clothing are all at the bottom of the pyramid and all these physical items require success, money or power to acquire. The first half of this book teaches you how to acquire physical needs by harnessing your mental state. The second half of the book, in Section III, focuses on how to acquire the mental state of self-actualization through growth and maturity.

Early in my motivational speaking career, a friend and fellow speaker told me most self-help and motivational wisdom comes from Psalms and Proverbs in the Christian Bible. He convinced me that most, if not all motivational speakers, me included, have been plagiarizing the Bible for all our speech and writing material since the beginning of time. I've come to believe this statement as majority, truth. I recommend all my mentees read Proverbs 3 everyday of their lives! It is full of wisdom and outlines how to live an exciting rewarding life. Many great authors I have recommended in this book have taken these biblical principles and words of wisdom to the next higher level. Thank God for these books of the Bible and for these authors who used their creative God-given genius to show us how to utilize these powerful principals. My goal is to suggest a way to combine the wisdom, techniques and concepts to help you build a strategic plan for your life.

My first real encounter with this new way of thinking, and proof that it possesses a considerable amount of validity, came shortly after I started practicing creative visualization. I was exploring numerous suggested techniques and started to experience some weird things in my private meditations. I was noticing more and more coincidences in my life, on a much higher frequency than ever before. I recall one incident that got my attention in a big way. I was spending a lot of time training for marathons and becoming somewhat bored with the same old long runs. I was looking for something to help change my exercise routine. I had a friend who suggested hiring a personal trainer to help me develop strength in all my muscle groups. I thought it might help me, so I decided to start looking for the perfect "personal trainer". I immediately started using the meditation techniques/creative visualization I was studying to assist me with my search.

Back in those days, I traveled extensively in my job and it was not uncommon for me to fly four or five times in a week. In my travels, I always tried to meet different and interesting people and usually flew Southwest Airlines, which had open seating and you could sit wherever you wished. One day on a flight to Los Angeles on Southwest Airlines, we had a stopover in Phoenix where I had to change planes. As I was getting on the flight in Houston, I was looking for someone interesting to talk with on the flight. I ended up sitting next to a very average looking guy, who turned out to be very interesting. We started talking halfway through the flight and we had a very in-depth conversation about emotional intelligence of all things. I was enthralled with his knowledge and we hit it off immediately. After about thirty minutes, he started to tell me about an interesting book he had been reading and it turned out to be the same book I was reading!! Wow, normally I would have thought this very strange, but a lot of people were starting to read bestselling books on self-help and I did not think much of it until I saw he was on page 121, the exact page number I was on! I pulled out my copy and showed him my book mark on page 121. Scary!! Interesting coincidence? We had a great laugh and continued to talk for the rest of the flight about this book. Turns out he was from Houston and was visiting relatives in San Francisco. We continued to talk the rest of the flight until I had to get off in Phoenix to catch my flight to LA. After the flight landed, I started to disembark and was half way down the aisle before I realized I never got his name. I stopped, turned around, went back to his seat, handed him a business card and invited him to continue our conversation over lunch when we both got back to Houston. He handed me his business card, and I left the plane.

When I got settled into my seat on the way to LA, I looked at his business card. It read: "John Corbin, Personal Trainer"!

P.S. "Whatever the mind dwells on will sooner or later come into existence or into your experience!"

P.P.S. "The inner world produces the outer world – Control your inner thoughts!"

Creative visualization works on a premise that everything in the universe is composed of only energy. If you break down all the physical structure of everything in the universe to its smallest component, it eventually disappears and at some point, exists as only energy. Electrons, protons, neutrons, etc. You are dealing with a transformation from a physical object to a mental/spiritual state, from solid material to a spiritual, esoteric state. At what point does it stop being physical and become mental/spiritual? This is an example of the dilemma of The Mind-Body Crossover mentioned earlier in this book. "I am not a human being, I'm a spiritual being". Once we understand this, we are growing in the right direction. I am by no means a pantheist, as I believe in a creator god. I believe that God created everything including energy, and we need to be aware of its existence and worship in the context of physics which he also created. I believe that prayer is energy. Reconfigured energy.

The same opportunity exists when you go the opposite direction of taking something spiritual, let's say a thought, and turning it into a physical object or physical occurrence/happening. The Bible teaches us whatever you can think of you can produce physically i.e. manifest in your life, both spiritually and physically and vice versa. In other words, Conceive, Believe, Achieve. Whatever you can conceive and believe, you can achieve! In the Book of Proverbs, chapter 23, verse 7: "As a man thinketh in his heart, so is he". Your mind in prayer and meditation is a very powerful communication tool. Today we know that changes in thinking can physically change the brain. Dr. Caroline Leaf, a communication pathologist, in her book SWITCH ON YOUR BRAIN, provides evidence that changes in thinking, change the brain and can affect behavioral change as well. Mind, does control matter! Ancient biblical scripture outlined for us thousands of years ago, what we are just starting to realize from extensive scientific study of the brain. This book shows the correlation between scripture and science. In her book she explains that we are wired for love, not fear and fear is a learned response. Many scientists characterize humans as "fear-based" due to built-in protection mechanisms in our brains to keep us safe. Leaf explains in her book our ability to change these perceptions by our thoughts. She explains: "Neuroplasticity by definition means the brain is malleable and adaptable, changing moment by moment of every day. Scientists are finally beginning to see the brain as having renewable characteristics and is no longer viewed as a machine that is hardwired early in life, unable to adapt, and wearing out with age. Today we know we can change the physical nature of our brain through our thinking and choosing." Even though we appear fear-based and fear-driven due to protection mechanisms in our brain, we in fact have the power to change that condition by our thoughts. In other words, thoughts do become things! A notable scientific discovery and self-help tool for those willing to implement change. Caroline Leaf's 21-Day Brain Detox Plan outlined in her book is consistent with many of the tools found in Tell Me What To Do. I encourage you to read her book: *Switch On Your Brain.* A very powerful documentation of how God, through his spirit, affects human behavior. If you are struggling with faith issues regarding belief in a higher power, this book will show you a way to fully understand how science and scripture work hand in hand for a better understanding of God and the universe. I encourage you to explore this concept for your own edification.

Psychologists and scientists say we only use a small portion of our brainpower - Probably less than 20% of our capacity. Some use a little more and some a little less, but no one reaches their full potential when it comes to utilizing the power of the brain. Our subconscious mind works overtime, utilizing a different operating system than our conscious mind utilizes. It's at work even when we are asleep.

The subconscious mind can't tell the difference between real and perceived. It works constantly trying to bring to fruition whatever you and I are capable of thinking. Think like a millionaire, tell yourself you are a millionaire and your subconscious will work overtime to take you there. (i.e. to manifest it in your life, in your reality, you become a millionaire).

A thought is only energy. Your thoughts will eventually create your reality. A thought is configured energy. Whatever you think about the most, you will become. Focus and think about what you want and your subconscious will work to manifest it in your reality, in your life. This is one of the reasons I stress to all my mentees the importance of what I call, Future Pacing. Thinking a lot about what you want the future to be like when you arrive there is a powerful tool. Your subconscious mind will take you there while you sleep. Having a clear picture of what you want out of life is necessary for living an exciting and joyful life. It's the reason we need a strategic plan for our lives. The plan forces us to consider what we want, and our subconscious mind helps us get there. Future pacing and building a strategic plan for your life are critical tools for success.

My business partner and spiritual mentor Ty Sudds, wrote the following about creative visualization and it helps codify the meaning of Future Pacing:

A thinking imagination is the substance in which all things are made and in fact in one's original state of mind, every thought permeates, penetrates and fills the imagination of probability. A thought produces the thing that is being imagined. Once a thought is put into form and given attention to detail, it can become physical material. Then, what we are thinking is created by following the pattern of the thought. We can literately create our thoughts to always express the results of our dominant thoughts. So, I know you've heard the Capital One commercial "What's in your wallet". We'll hear this. "What's in your thought". Uuuuummm!!! Copyright Ty Sudds 2015. All Rights Reserved. Proverbs 23:7.

Dr. Jim Will, a close friend and mentor, has taken these concepts to another level by exploring our "negative" and "positive" self-talk. His work on our thought processes is an eye-opening discussion on how critical it is to control our thoughts, because our subconscious can't tell what's real and what's not. The observation here is: Think positive thoughts and you will manifest positive results. Think negative thoughts and you will manifest negative results. Yikes!! Be careful! Watch what you are thinking! Never catch yourself saying something is impossible. Always think in possibilities. Reminds me of one of my favorite quotes:

"Impossible is just a big word thrown around by small men who find it easier to live in the world they've been given than to explore the power they have to change it. Impossible is not a fact. It's an opinion. Impossible is not a declaration. It's a dare. Impossible is potential. Impossible is temporary. Impossible is nothing."

— Muhammad Ali, born Cassius Marcellus Clay, Jr., American professional boxer

THE GREAT "I AM" EXERCISE

This simple assignment is consistent with the information given in this book regarding the subconscious mind and how we can manifest our thoughts into reality by what we think, say, profess and write. I call this, "speaking into existence", our most desired character attributes. Creative visualization tells us we become what we focus on and what we profess out of our mouth and think in our mind. This is a technique in positive self-talk that utilizes the mind body crossover discussed earlier. i.e. Have a thought and physically put it on paper. I encourage you to undertake this assignment for proof of how your subconscious mind will lead you to manifestation even while you sleep. This is a short assignment that takes about ten minutes to initiate but is very powerful and life changing. The Christian and Jewish religion use a similar term to identity their creator god. Their Godhead is acknowledged and identified as "I Am". Completion of this exercise won't make you as powerful as the ancient scriptures connotation of God, but it will bring to your reality the power of this exercise and the phenomenal power you possess within your subconscious mind. My mentees call this exercise The List of 77. By the way, most people acknowledge 7 as a very powerful and lucky number! Seven is the number of completeness and perfection, (both physical and spiritual). Proceed.

Grab an 8.5 X 11 paper tablet with lines and fill up three pages, approximately 77 items, with "I am" statements about your factual personality and future desires you would like to manifest in your life. Looks like this:

I am free of bad habits

I am positive all the time

I am designed to make right choices

I am filled with peace

I am a spirit filled Christian

I am a great father

I am designed for intellectual thought

I am fearless

I am wired for love

I am a great friend

I am always on time

I am made in Gods image

I am a prayer warrior

I am sexually pure

I am free of guilt and shame

I am free of rejection and hurt

I am content with my God

I am healthy

I am not a victim

I am free of over-analyzing

I am not a quitter

I am not wounded

I am frugal with my money

I am a great planner

I am going to make great decisions

I am going to pray for others every day

I am smiling when I awake in the morning

I am faithful to my husband

I am creating my reality through my thoughts

I am a self-starter

I am free of all fear

I am a goal setter

I am capable of forgiveness

I am in a sacred marriage

I am family focused

I am worry free

I am strong

I am renewing my brain by my positive thoughts

I am consciously directing and controlling my thoughts

I am filled with joy

Etc. etc. etc. Get the idea? Keep the list by your night stand. Every night right before you turn out the light and go to sleep whisper out loud each of the 77 statements. Repeat this for 77 days. The power of the assignment will be revealed. This is one of the most powerful tools to help manifest positive, permanent change. Reading them out loud is important as you will learn later in this book when we discuss vibration and the power produced when we manipulate and transform energy, i.e. thoughts. Stay tuned.

PRAYER: ENERGY, VIBRATION, MIRACLES, NON-MIRACLES

As mentioned earlier, a thought is only configured energy. Prayer is a group of thoughts placed together forming a higher set of energies. Meditation likewise. Science says that you cannot destroy energy, you can only reconfigure it. The importance of prayer and meditation cannot be underestimated due to this fact of nature. People who think positive thoughts are known to have better "luck" than people who think negative thoughts. Likes attract likes. You manifest, or you become, what you think about most.

> "People who pray for miracles usually don't get miracles . . . but people who pray for courage, for strength to bear the unbearable, for the grace to remember what they have left instead of what they have lost, very often find their prayers answered . . . their prayers helped them tap hidden reserves of faith and courage which were not available to them before."
>
> — Harold Samuel Kushner,
> American Rabbi and author

I love this quote! It codifies for me the realities of life, the realities of prayer and the realities of miracles in one statement. As a Christian, I have experienced very few extraordinary miracles, but I have experienced a lot of non-miracles. What do I mean by this? Sound ambiguous? Sound confusing? What I'm referring to is the reality that sometimes our prayers are answered, sometimes they are never answered, sometimes we are not aware that they are answered, sometimes they are answered in a form we don't anticipate, and sometimes they are answered years after we pray for them. Many times, we have forgotten we even prayed for them to be answered in the first place.

Saying prayers out loud creates a vibration when we speak. Speaking out loud transforms the vibration to another form of energy that goes out into the universe. Many Christians believe you speak (verbally) into existence, your desired result, in a prayer petition to God. Christian scripture, Matthew 18:20 says: "For where two or three gather together in My name, there am I with them." This passage from the Christian Bible is in reference to group prayer.

As mentioned earlier, I have only seen a few events that I would classify as miracles during my lifetime. As a Christian, I choose to believe they are the result of Intense Faith in a higher power who is intervening in the lives of those affected because of intense prayer. Obviously, a non-believer or a person of little faith can never be sure if one is observing a coincidence or observing divine intervention. As a believer, I was fortunate to observe one such incident several years ago when a close friend and former co-worker, Jeff Webb was diagnosed with cancer. I firmly believe I saw the hand of God intervene. I also believe I saw the power of positive self-talk and the power of positive thinking.

I got a call from a friend and former co-worker, Tim Canon, one of Jeff's close friends one afternoon, informing me of Jeff's predicament. I was very distraught, as Jeff was a longtime friend, and I picked up the phone and called him immediately. At the time of the occurrence, I was a member of a group of Prayer Warriors started by Mike Jackson, who was a close Christian friend I met on a spiritual retreat called The Walk to Emmaus, years earlier. Our group of five prayer warriors would go and pray verbally over terminally ill patients whenever requested. Mike Jackson, the founder of the team, was a big believer in speaking/praying verbally in corporate prayer over ill patients. I told Jeff about our group of prayer warriors, and he invited us to come pray over him at his house.

We convened at Jeff's house with his wife Shirley one afternoon, and he told us what was going on with his situation. He explained that after his first colonoscopy at age 54, he was diagnosed with stage 1 colon cancer. Jeff and Shirley went to the consultation regarding the results of the new P.E.T. scan. At the time, he was not really alarmed, thinking a small tumor needed to be removed. The doctor proceeded to tell Jeff and Shirley that the scan revealed a large cancerous tumor the size of a walnut in Jeff's colon that needed to be removed. He decided to move to M. D. Anderson Cancer Center in Houston because of their reputation as one of the world's leading cancer centers. The doctors at M. D. Anderson ran their own set of tests with upgraded technology. A week later the new test results were in. They proceeded to show them the P.E.T. scan up on a screen for them to see the bright pink image of the tumor. While the physician was pointing out the location of the tumor, Jeff noticed a multitude of colorful, purple, circular disks above the colon. Jeff immediately inquired what they represented. The doctor rather stoically said: "This is the reason we asked you to bring Shirley." Yikes! He proceeded to tell Jeff and Shirley that there were over forty individual tumors found on his liver. Jeff says he immediately knew this was not good and in slow motion started to pass out and said he heard Shirley starting to cry before he hit floor. Stage four colon cancer!

The power of positive self-talk and the power of positive thinking is what I saw next out of Jeff and Shirley over the next 6-9 months, in addition to an extraordinary faith in a Higher

Power. I saw Jeff and Shirley make a mega leap to Spiritual Maturity which I will explain in a later chapter.

After Jeff finished telling his story, our Prayer Warriors gathered around Jeff and Shirley and prayed over them about twenty minutes. These were all individually spoken prayers, verbally exclaimed by the five warriors with intensity and verbal furor.

The following week after the prayer session and after undergoing 5 months of chemo therapy, Jeff was scheduled for his first surgery to have the tumor in his colon removed. That surgery would be followed by surgery on his liver to hopefully remove the additional tumors. The liver is the only organ in your body that self regenerates. In theory, you could remove the tumors and the organ would regenerate new tissue. You must however leave a big enough piece of the original liver to allow it to grow back. This was the plan. A laborious process, but survival is possible with a little luck.

Next comes the unbelievable! The surgeon goes in to remove the tumor in the colon a week after the prayer session and can find no evidence of the tumor in Jeff's colon!!! (Surgeon cannot explain and calls the event unexplainable)!

Next comes the miracle - Again! After several months of recovery, the surgeon goes in to start removal of the tumors in Jeff's liver. Only small charred pieces of tissue can be found where the tumors were located! (Surgeon says it's one in a million, has no explanation and calls it a miracle).

Throughout the entire ordeal, I never saw Jeff or Shirley doubt the prospects of his absolute survival! There was a lot of prayer and lot of positive vibes by friends, loved ones and Jeff and Shirley. Today, Jeff's colon and liver are cancer free and he has joined our Prayer Warriors on several occasions to pray over other terminally ill patients.

I'm not sure what I witnessed! Was this the power of GOD? Was this the power of prayer? The power of positive thinking? The power of positive self-talk? The power of creative visualization? All the above? You decide.

CHAPTER SUMMARY

 GOLDEN NUGGETS:

- "Creative visualization is the technique of using your imagination to create what you want in your life." -- Shakti Gawain.

- The Mind-Body Crossover is a term coined to help explain a system I've created to help individuals acquire superior goal achievement.

- Once you fully understand how your subconscious mind works, you can make mega leaps in your quest for financial freedom and living a life full of purpose, joy and peace while expanding your self-awareness.

- "Whatever the mind dwells on will sooner or later come into existence or into your experience!"

- Mind, does control matter!

- Ancient biblical scripture outlined for us thousands of years ago, what we are just starting to realize from extensive scientific study of the brain.

- If you are struggling with faith issues regarding belief in a higher power, this book will show you a way to fully understand how science and scripture work hand in hand for a better understanding of God and the universe.

- The subconscious mind can't tell the difference between real and perceived. It works constantly trying to bring to fruition whatever you and I are capable of thinking. It is at work while we sleep. Very powerful.

- Your thoughts will eventually create your reality. Positive or negative.

- A thought is only configured energy. Prayer is a group of thoughts placed together forming a higher set of energies.

- People who think positive thoughts have better luck than people who think negative thoughts. Likes attract likes. Think negative thoughts, and you will manifest negative results. Watch what you are thinking!

- Saying prayers out loud creates a vibration. Speaking out loud transforms the vibration to another form of energy that goes out into the universe, searching for what you are praying. Consider praying out loud. It works.

- Hesitation kills!

ACTION ITEMS: (TELL ME WHAT TO DO)

- Set reminders on your phone or calendar to think only positive thoughts every day, to be positive every day and to smile more every day.
- Complete your List of 77 – The Great I Am Exercise.
- Read aloud your list of 77 items for 77 nights in a row before you go to sleep.

CHAPTER FIVE

UNIQUE ABILITY

I often start many speaking presentations by asking the audience: "How many of you know your unique ability?" Most people have a somewhat inquisitive look when the question is asked. What does unique ability mean? Does it mean what you are good at? Is it the results you get when taking a personality profile/assessment test? How do you define unique ability? Here is my definition: Unique ability means knowing what you personally can do, that the other 6-7 billion people on earth cannot do. It's what is unique to only you.

I'm convinced that self-discovery and self-awareness is the key to success and joy! It all starts with the search for your unique ability. You can't hope to grow if you do not know the answer to this question. Unfortunately, very few people know the answer, or seek to know the answer. The emotionally mature and intuitive person is searching for the answer all their life. If you want to experience passion and true joy in your life, you first must know who you are, and what makes you tick. You must know your unique ability if you want to have purpose, passion and success in your life. Proverbs 18:16 in the Christian Bible has this scripture: A man's gift maketh room for him, and bringeth him before great men.

I continuously mentor fifteen to twenty young professionals, most of whom are under the age of thirty-five. One of their first assignments is to work on discovering their unique ability. I recommend my mentees start by taking as many personality profile tests as possible. "Strengths Finder 2.0" by Rath is my recommendation for an economical test with great value. Buy this book and you get the test for free. There are numerous free tests available on the internet that also will give you some insight into your own personality. It can be a lot of fun and a very informative experience.

In the mid 1990's I took a profile test that changed my life and helped further define my unique ability in a profound way. Many people in the industry consider it the Rolls Royce of personality/aptitude tests, known as The Birkman Method. I had the good fortune of meeting the founder of the organization Dr. Roger Birkman in 1997. He was a very astute, quiet, unassuming individual that projected instant credibility and wisdom. I sensed a unique spiritual persona when in his company. After taking his profile test I was amazed at the accuracy of the results and was convinced that Dr. Birkman must have been God inspired to create such an amazing tool. He has since died, but I learned more about myself, my emotions and my personality than from any other person or method of testing. I encourage you to explore his testing methods for a dead-on assessment of who you are and how you think, act and react. You will be amazed. A true God Wink! (See: The Beautiful Life of Roger Birkman). www.loci.international.com/white papers/The Beautiful Mind of Roger Birkman. (See The Relational 360 – www. loci.international.com/toolsofthought/The LOCI Relationship 360).

Knowing how and what other people think about you, is the first step in discovering your unique ability. As human beings, we are all "projecting" every waking hour. We are quite often not aware of how we project ourselves to others and how we are perceived by others. Most of us are not even aware of our facial expressions much less our body language.

Research indicates that most of us only understand about 85% of our own personality. Many things about ourselves that are hidden from our own consciousness. Some research argues that the percentage we know about ourselves is much smaller than the quoted 85%. Getting input from others is a valuable tool that should not be overlooked. To start the discovery process, I recommend my students start by sending out about 35-40 emails to close friends, associates and relatives they value and trust, people who they think know them best. I recommend they include parents, siblings, close friends, relatives, business associates, sorority and fraternity friends, spiritual advisors (pastor, rabbi, priest) and anyone else who has known them for an extended period. The email should/could read as follows:

> "Janet, I just hired a new personal coach who has given me an interesting assignment to assist in my personal growth. I'm in the process of reevaluating my life, my current position and career, to grow and expand my sphere of influence, my own self-awareness and my personal/professional development. I am looking for feedback from a select group of close friends and associates for an honest assessment, and you are high on my list. I would appreciate you taking a few minutes and tell me what you perceive to be my "Unique Ability". Please don't get hung up on the definition of unique ability, just give me your best assessment. My ego is prepared to accept the positive and negative. I just need and appreciate your honest input. Thanks, in advance for your honest feedback. Please send via return email. I appreciate you!"

Get ready for some interesting comments. Most of us will generally agree with the results of a personality profile test if we take them with an honest and open sincerity. However, most of us are not aware of our mental scotomas. What's a scotoma? Definition: field of vision consisting of a partially diminished or entirely degenerated visual acuity that is surrounded by a field of normal – or relatively well-preserved–vision. I first heard this term from a well-known consultant/motivational trainer, Dr. Jim Will, mentioned earlier. (I highly recommend Jim as a speaker, coach, personal or business consultant - Power Of Self Talk: www.jimwillphd.com).

Basically, a mental scotoma is a blind spot we are not aware of personally. Usually others see it, but we can't or don't see it. Most of us are not aware that we are "projecting" every moment, all day, every day, to everybody we meet. We are not aware of our projection, (our body language, our facial expressions, etc.) but everyone else gets a sense and opinion of who and what we are by these projections. Naturally, we do not necessarily see our own projection, but everyone else does. These unknown scotomas say a lot about us.

When you start to receive return emails from your friends you will more than likely start to discover some of your own scotomas. Ninety percent of what you read from your friends/associates you will agree with without exception. Then out of the blue, someone will say something about your unique ability that you will vehemently disagree with, as you do not recognize the "personality trait" mentioned. Take those comments seriously as they are telling you something you do not know about yourself! It is probably factual if you see the trait mentioned by others, in your email group of friends and associates. It might go something like this: "Sandy, I think your unique ability has to do with your outgoing personality. You are such a glamorous, outgoing person and everyone just loves being around you. You have a type A personality and you always seem driven to succeed. I also notice that you seem to enjoy abusing small animals." What? Abuse small animals you say? Who wrote this??!!?? In disagreement and disgust, you move on, as obviously, this person has a skewed opinion of you, and they really don't know you at all! You proceed to read the other emails from your friends. The next ten emails seem very normal, and you tend to agree with what is expressed. Then you open the 22nd email and it reads as: "Sandy I think your unique ability has to do with your willingness to help other people. I like the way you can get along with almost anyone. You are such a gregarious and outgoing person, and everyone seems drawn to you. You have a great personality, and you always seem driven to outpace the competition. I also notice that you seem to enjoy abusing small animals." Yikes!

Obviously, this is a funny and extreme example to prove a point. Whenever, more than one person identifies the same trait that you are certain you don't possess--Wake up! It's a mental scotoma. You are projecting. You just learned something very valuable about yourself that you did not previously know. You are starting to learn more about yourself and your unique ability.

The quest for knowing your unique ability is never ending as it continues to grow and change as you grow and change. However, the core basis of your unique ability rarely changes and that is what you want to discover. Most of us can identify about 85-90% of our unique ability, but some nuances continue to grow and develop as we get older. I would hope that you could write a statement about your unique ability after finishing the exercises in this book, i.e. emails to friends, personality tests, etc.

Here is my evolving statement about my personal unique ability to date:

> "I have passion for helping individuals discover their unique ability and to help them use this knowledge to grow towards spiritual maturity. I am gifted with an ability to motivate individuals to discover and recognize their unique talents, desires, shortcomings, character defects and abilities. My positive mental attitude and speaking ability are clear attributes of my own unique ability. Helping others discover their passion so they can find and grow towards their own maturity and unique ability is a major part of my own unique ability."

This exercise, along with additional personality profile tests, will help you discover and refine your unique ability. Its discovery, is the only way to have true passion for what you attempt and be truly happy in all seven areas of your life. Continue the exploration. It's well worth the discovery.

CHAPTER SUMMARY

 ## GOLDEN NUGGETS:

- "Unique Ability" means knowing what you personally can do that the other 6-7 billion people on earth cannot do.

- If you want to experience passion and true joy in your life, you first must know who you are, and what makes you tick.

- Many people in the industry consider it the Rolls Royce of personality/aptitude tests, known as The Birkman Method.

- As human beings, we are all "projecting" every waking hour. We are quite often not aware of how we project ourselves and how we are perceived by others.

- A mental scotoma is a blind spot we are not aware of personally.

- The quest for knowing your unique ability is never ending as it continues to grow and change as you do.

- Hesitation kills!

ACTION ITEMS: (TELL ME WHAT TO DO)

- Make a list of 15 additional traits from Chapter One that you think further identify some of your unique ability.
- Send out an email to 20-30 of your closest friends as outlined.
- After reviewing responses from your email outlined above, make your first attempt at writing a paragraph about your unique ability as outlined on the previous page.

CHAPTER SIX

PERSONALITY PROFILES

Understanding your personality is critical to building a strategic plan for your life. One of the first steps in solving the success, money, power – challenge, mentioned earlier. Most of your personality is established and locked in before you are three years old. Medical science suggests that 80% of your personality markers are formed while you are still in your mother's womb. Medical science and technology also says you can't change your personality in any meaningful way after the age of three or four, as it is locked in your DNA. If you take a good personality profile/assessment test when you are seventeen and then again when you are seventy-seven you will come within 3 percentage points because it is a part of your DNA that can't be changed. We can only change our habits. (Social scientists continue to debate the nurture/nature issue. While I am taking a strong "Nature" approach I am mindful and informed by new neuroscience challenges that argue for a strong "Nurture" approach - see Barrett) See How Emotions are Made: The Secret Life of the Brain by Lisa Feldman Barret.

My parents always encouraged me to have "passion" for whatever I attempted in life. They did not, unfortunately, tell me how to have passion or how to discover it. They just said, be passionate! Understanding and knowing your own personality type is very valuable for you to experience a lot of peace, joy, success and contentment in life. It's the first step to finding your real passion.

I'm always amazed that more emphasis is not given to exploring personality traits. Many parents don't understand they cannot control and manipulate their children's personalities. I encourage all parents to start testing their children at an early age to determine how they are wired. I often see parents who ignore this and raise miserably discontented children. Google: Birkman Testing Children. As a wise adult, I encourage you to also take a good personality test in a continuing effort to help find your unique ability and fully define your passion. Finding your passion should be easy. It's what you love to do more than anything else in the world. It's what you would do for free! It's different from "Unique Ability" but they work in concert with one another. Your passion exists as a form of energy inside your unique ability. It stays with you continuously at work, at home, at play! It never leaves.

If you want to be highly successful and emotionally content, I believe you must understand your personality type. Most personality exams test for numerous different characteristics and traits (introvert, extrovert, passive, aggressive, impulsive, high attention to detail, low attention to detail, etc.). This is a highly technical field and much too complicated to fully explore in this book, but I do want to stress the basics for your personal growth and growth of your loved ones. Most personality tests today are 95 to 100% accurate when taken in the correct setting with proper supervision. As mentioned previously I recommend Birkman Testing as the most comprehensive assessment tool on the market. The importance of this testing can be better understood through the following two examples.

EXAMPLE #1:

Cameron's father is the owner of one of the largest CPA firms in the city and wants his son to head up the audit department at his firm after Cameron graduates from college. The father does not understand the importance of personality profiling and never tests his son to ascertain his highest and best capabilities. Most people will agree that accounting requires a considerable amount of high attention to detail. After many false starts at establishing a career, Cameron eventually takes a personality profile test. The results are very revealing. On a scale of 1-10, Cameron scores a 1 on attention to detail. Obviously, he should not pursue a career where high attention to detail is required. Thousands, if not millions of people make similar mistakes. I encourage you to take a personality test to help determine your unique ability. There are numerous free tests on the internet and some very sophisticated tests that can give you a lot of insight into your strengths and weaknesses and save you a lot of grief. To have passion for what you attempt in life, you must work inside your personality profile.

It is also critical to fully understand the importance of testing and how the results can be very helpful, when taken with a serious attitude. We need to understand the importance of being honest on the test that there are no right or wrong answers, and that the results can be totally confidential if requested. The main thing is to get a good accurate test, taken during an emotionally static time and in a non-threatening environment. Never take a test after a big meal to prevent glucose from skewing the results, and always choose a time of day when you are higher on your personal emotional scale. Most companies that sell profile tests have a very well defined and well explained set of rules and instructions for taking the test. It is critical not to ignore or overlook these recommended instructions.

EXAMPLE #2

This example might help better explain the intricacies of personality testing and increased awareness of the fallacy of preconceived notions about certain personality characteristics. I have interviewed and hired people in most every position within a company and always use an appropriate profile test to help determine capability and potential for success. I have hired or assisted in the hiring of over 300 individuals, of which over 145 were commercial real estate brokers. Highly successful commercial real estate brokers are a very rare breed. I have learned over the years that I can test for only three personality traits if I want to acquire only brokers that will make a lot of money. This is not to say, that making a lot of money should be the driving force behind hiring. Hiring only "money-makers" can be a recipe for disaster. It is only being discussed to give you a better understanding of the testing process and the meaning behind what makes certain personalities "tick"!

There are functional and dysfunctional individuals in every area of employment and life in general. Dysfunctional individuals can serve a much-needed dynamic in certain circumstances. Directors of large brokerage organizations will tell you that managing brokers is like trying to herd cats up a hill! Most successful brokers are highly competitive and argumentative by nature (i.e. their profiles) and you need to hire a complementary set of individuals to counter these strong personalities if you want to have a high functioning team. The Birkman Method, mentioned earlier, is worth its weight in gold when undertaking this assignment.

Early in my career, as a managing director of commercial real estate brokers, I learned that you could hire a certain kind of dysfunctional individual, if your only concern was producing high profits, and you were not concerned with real qualities, like ethics and morals, etc. If you want to have high dollar producing teams, you need to hire a certain number of what I call dysfunctional kill-to-eat brokers. All 100% commissioned brokers can be defined as kill-to-eat brokers. That means they don't make any money, unless they sell something. i.e. You must "kill" something, if you want to eat! That does not mean all brokers are dysfunctional. To the contrary, most are highly functional, moral and ethical individuals.

In the early eighties, Houston was booming, and a lot of people were making a lot of money in oil and gas and commercial real estate development was going wild. I was working for one of the top commercial real estate firms in the city when given an opportunity to start my own operation with Rubloff, out of Chicago, founded in the 1930's by Arthur Rubloff, a highly successful real estate entrepreneur and showman. It was one of the largest commercial real estate firms in the country, and I could not believe my good fortune. They were looking for a new managing director in Houston, and I landed the job. It gave me an opportunity to hire my own people and build an organization. My personality profiling experience gave me an interesting perspective in hiring "kill-to-eat" brokers. I went to work for Arthur Rubloff's protégé, a marketing and sales guru by the name of Howard Weinstein who was known as the King of "Schmooze." (A Yiddish term that comes from the Yiddish shmuesn-which means to chat with idle conversation/talk to include "rumors"). He was truly an extraordinary salesman and gifted leader with an impeccable reputation for excellence and performance.

I learned a lot from Howard including a huge sense of urgency to perform. Howard liked moving at the speed of light and was anxious to grow the company. For job security, it was imperative that I move quickly and build a profitable organization in the shortest amount of time. I set out immediately to hire some high-performance brokers. When I started hiring brokers, I made an interesting discovery about personalities, which helps prove a point about the need to understand what makes people tick.

Here are three personality characteristics unique to dysfunctional highly successful, kill-to-eat brokers who make a lot of money: 1) Attention to detail, 2) Impulsivity and 3) Emotional Quotient. If I were to ask you how to rate these three characteristics for a person to be a highly successful, kill-to-eat salesman, how would you rate each of these characteristics? Do they have high attention to detail or low attention to detail? What about Impulsivity – High or Low? What about Emotional Quotient – High or Low? Very rarely have I seen people answer correctly regarding all three of these traits for high performing kill-to-eat brokers.

High Attention to Detail: Meaning = They dot every "I" and cross every "T" – very meticulous and careful about getting all the details correct. Answer is: Kill-to-eat brokers rate very low in this category. They are only interested in getting the deal done as soon as possible and getting paid. They are usually insecure and think that they are only as good as their next deal and want to move on quickly.

Impulsivity: Meaning = They can make quick decisions without a lot of careful thought. Answer is: Very High. They are only interested in getting the deal done as soon as possible and getting paid. They tend to act quickly. When they drive down the freeway and see a new "For Sale" sign on a piece of property, they usually pick up their phone immediately and call the co-op broker before they pass the sign. They are highly impulsive.

Emotional Quotient: Meaning = They are very emotionally aware. They can cry when they hear their college fight song. They can easily hug another person of the same sex. Answer is: Very Low. Most kill-to-eat brokers are homophobic and refuse to show any emotional display of any kind, regardless of circumstance, due to being fear-based and insecure.

The answers to these traits listed above might surprise you, but they are indicative that often we do not fully understand what truly makes people tick.

I use this testing technique when I'm trying to quickly hire big profit producers. A good managing director will only have a few of these type individuals in his organization if he wants to maintain a functioning group. The example does however, outline the need to understand personality profiling to solve a certain type of problem.

OBSERVING CHILDREN - TEACHES PROFILING

When you understand how children function, you start to learn a lot about profiling and a lot about yourself as well. What was your childhood like? Parents take notes! Your children's success in life is a direct result of your parenting and a direct reflection of your personal competency and a demonstration of your legacy. A direct result of your ability to communicate and understand. Your ability to listen.

It's important for us to understand how our parents raised us to fully understand how we think, act and react. Some "helicopter parents" try to fix everything for their kids which can result in an entitlement mentality and become quite destructive. This can also be very detrimental to emotional growth. Are you a product of helicopter parents? Do you have an entitlement mentality? The best parents learn to listen and create an atmosphere for children to learn on their own and motivate themselves. These parents tell their children they can accomplish anything, speaking reality into existence!

We are all products of our upbringing which ultimately shapes who we become later in life. It's the parents' job to help children understand that they have God-given gifts. It's also the parents' responsibility to help the child discover their gifts and to give children confidence that they are, in fact, different and OK, from other kids. You need to "pour into" your children! Pour, Pour, Pour!! Every day, every day, every day! Tell them how smart they are. Tell them how beautiful they are, daily! Hug them every day. Tell them you love them - every day! Tell them they can be anything they want to be with hard work - every day! Then create an atmosphere where they can feel secure always and they will learn on their own! Children need to feel secure to discover their own gifts. When you speak these truths out loud to your children, it gives the words energy and power. The vibration of your words is the first step to manifesting a simple statement into a reality, as discussed in chapter four on Creative Visualization. Speak positive messages to your children loudly and often. Most Montessori Schools focus on using positive verbal affirmations and reinforcement and place special focus on letting children gravitate to their individual unique ability.

Example: Little Sally comes home frustrated after school because her best friend Connie is making straight A's in Algebra. Sally is having trouble understanding anything about numbers and feels vastly inferior to Connie. Her parents decide to put Sally through some personality testing and find that she scores very high in art, reading, acting and writing, but scores low in math skills and science. In a Montessori setting, students can gravitate and focus on their individual interests. Once this discovery is made, Sally stops focusing on areas where her ability does not correspond to her interest. She stops taking math and science courses, other than the basics, and turns her attention to art, acting, reading, etc. Her parents start to verbally reinforce her individual abilities, she starts to excel in these subjects, and her self-esteem and self-worth skyrocket because she is finally working and operating inside her profile.

Are you working inside your profile? It is very important that we work, live and play inside our personality profiles and our unique abilities. It's also important for us and our children to discover our gifts through proper encouragement, testing and verbal affirmation. Consider putting your children in Montessori Schools or other similar programs if you want them to have passion for what they attempt in life and to be self-confident and full of life. Also, consider this information for your own life. Get your kids and yourself, tested!

There are several other recommended ideas to help grow highly productive, passionate and self-sustaining children. Their success is a major statement about your success! If you want your children to be leaders and entrepreneurial spirited individuals, I recommend involvement in certain activities at an early age, regardless of personality type.

There is little you can do to change one's personality profile after the age of three or four, but there are habits you can instill that will help shape character. In other words, IQ's are set and static by age 3-4, but emotional quotient (EQ) can improve with education. A recent survey of highly successful, goal-oriented individuals discovered that successful individuals were involved in certain activities during childhood that expanded their knowledge of the world and helped grow and expand their

EQ's. There were two common threads these individuals experienced growing up. They were involved in scouting programs and children-run businesses. Were you involved in either of these activities as a child? At the top of the achievement ladder were Eagle Scouts and Kool-Aid Stand aficionados! It was noted, children involved in these two activities were highly successful, goal oriented, well rounded individuals in their working careers. These individuals had several common markers in their childhood. If you were involved in these activities growing up, it shows something about you. It's worthy to note most scouting programs promote goal setting through the acquisition of merit badges. Goal setting is a well-known attribute of highly successful people. Establishing and operating a Kool-Aid stand as a young child requires of number of learned entrepreneurial skills. (Building a stand, making a product, pricing a product, customer interaction, marketing, advertising, etc.). It teaches the basics of running an entire business which can be very valuable in life regardless if you or a business person, a mother, a coach, a teacher, a doctor, a lawyer, a politician, an Indian Chief, etc. Building and operating a Kool-Aid stand builds self-esteem and self-confidence immediately. We had lots of Kool-Aid stands at the Dahse House!

Here are a few other tidbits for your children's success, that will ultimately manifest into your own success. Talk to them at an early age about sex, drugs and rock-n-roll. Today, pornography is killing innocence in our children at an alarming rate. You must be very vigilant to stop this insidious disease and protect your love ones and yourself, as I'm talking to adults as well as children. Pornography is recognized as one of the most powerful addictions. It is on the level of crack cocaine and meth! Addiction changes the brain's communication pathways. The human brain continues to create new neurons and form neural pathways throughout our entire lifespan. These neurons are dynamic cells that are constantly adapting to changing circumstances. Brain scans of individuals addicted to pornography show neural pathways larger than crack cocaine addicts! Be aware that you and your children are not alone in this situation and be aware of the traps of addiction and how to deal with peer pressure. This applies to adults as well as children! Once your children know you really care, because of your questioning and caring, they will bring issues to you regardless of the topic. Start this practice in early childhood and continue it through puberty and young adulthood. It will never feel awkward or uncomfortable if you start at an early age. Do not ignore pornography! It's destroying unaware adults and young children all over the world. Check their computers, their electronic games, their emails and their texts continually! Today, it is common practice for young children to send inappropriate nude photos to the opposite sex starting at a very early age. Obviously, addicted adults know the insidiousness of the addiction once they are hooked. Eight out of ten male adults look at some pornography. You must be vigilant, very vigilant! There are great twelve step programs that deal with this addiction.

A quick word about HOPE. It's imperative to be "positive" with your children always, as hopelessness is the worst thing that can happen to a child or adult. It's much worse than sadness, which you can usually deal with more easily. Hopelessness issues usually manifest themselves due to a lack of positive interaction with peers. You need to be aware of the dangers of too much time on electronic games and devices. Very dangerous! Severely restrict time in front of a screen for you and your children. It is very important to develop proper social skills at an early age and computer electronics are causing all kinds of maladies in young adults and our children. Lack of social interaction with other humans is causing emotional behavior problems for young and old alike. Beware! Specialists in this field say we should limit exposure to electronic games to a maximum of an hour a day.

Connectivity is vital to proper socialization of all humans, young and old. Interaction on a personal level, requiring eye contact and physical interaction like listening are skills that must be developed early on in development. It's important that we all are listened to and that we learn to listen to others as well. Listening to others broadens our connection/connectivity. It is critical to emotional health!

Two parting comments dealing with trust and maturity. I'm fortunate to have two highly successful children who I believe are properly socialized and well adjusted. I attribute most of this success to their mother's exceptional parenting skills and two decisions we made together as a couple about their continuing education once they were preparing to leave the nest. Here are the comments:

FIRST COMMENT

Our children always had a curfew as teenagers. It was strictly monitored and enforced when they were in high school. When each child graduated from their junior year in high school we called them into a serious conversation. We told them that their senior year in high school would be curfew free! Wow, you should have seen the reaction! Both children were shocked! We explained they would be allowed to stay out if they wanted if they were engaged in healthy activities. We further explained they always had to call no later than midnight, if they were not going to be home. We spent a considerable amount of time laying the ground rules and explained our reasoning behind the action. It was a very serious conversation about our trust and our belief that they would always act responsibly. This act turned out to be the most important thing we did getting them ready to go to college and eventually step out into the real world. They started to take 100% responsibility for what happened to them in life, something we will discuss in more detail later in this book. A powerful move!

P.S. I believe we only received two calls from each child during their senior year!! Once we showed trust in their ability to make their own decisions, they never abused the privilege.

SECOND COMMENT

We informed both of our children, they would be required to attend college overseas for at least a semester. We were concerned that they learn about what was going on in the real world. This proved to be very beneficial for social enlightenment. Surprisingly, my son Matt was a little reluctant when he first heard about this requirement but ended up spending a semester or two at Vienna School of Economics in Austria. His sister on the other hand, was raring to go after she saw how much fun her brother was having, and she attended college in Barcelona, Spain. Today they are both travel maniacs and well versed/educated about different cultures because of their extensive travel. If you are a young adult and not settled into a career, I would encourage you to explore the possibility of traveling overseas for three or four months before you look for a job.

Giving our children the ability to make their own decisions about curfews gave them a confidence about their abilities to make good decisions on their own. It also demonstrated that we trusted them to make good decisions. We did this their senior year in high school, so we could be available to help in the event they made a bad decision and needed our help. Overseas travel taught them a lot about unsupervised personal responsibility. They made mega leaps in their personal growth by having to take 100% responsibility for their actions overseas. They realized their parents weren't around to pick them up if they made a mistake overseas. I encourage you to consider these two suggestions for helping to make mega leaps and grow to maturity.

CHAPTER SUMMARY

♣ GOLDEN NUGGETS:

- Understanding your personality is critical to building a strategic plan for your life.

- To be highly successful and emotionally content, I believe you must understand what type of personality you possess.

- Most personality tests today are 95 to 100% accurate when taken in the correct setting with proper supervision.

- There are functional and dysfunctional individuals in every area of employment and life in general.

- Stop fixing everything for your kids. Just listen and create an atmosphere for them to learn on their own and where they can learn to motivate themselves. Teach them to respect others and be kind to the less fortunate.

- Tell your kids they can accomplish anything. It speaks reality into existence! Tell yourself the same thing!

- Giving our children the ability to make their own decisions about curfews gave them confidence in their own abilities to make good decisions.

- We all make mega leaps in our personal growth by taking 100% responsibility for our actions.

- Hesitation kills!

ACTION ITEMS: (TELL ME WHAT TO DO)

- Surf the internet to find and take three different personality profile tests. Take the tests and keep the results. We will use them later.

CHAPTER SEVEN

THE LIST OF 500

I've been a keynote speaker professionally for over forty years. My most requested topic is: How to Build a Strategic Plan for Your Life. It is a key component of my system and a lot of fun if you are serious about living life to the fullest. The list of 500 is the starting point for constructing the Strategic Plan. It is a process to help you identify your wants, needs and desires in all seven areas of your life. A strategic plan for your life must address these seven areas.

The List of 500 is how you start to identify these items and start the imprinting process in your mind. Take this assignment seriously, as it is the starting point of acquiring everything you want in life. Remember that writing down a thought, i.e. picking up a pen or a pencil and writing out a thought on a piece of paper, brings it to fruition faster than just thinking about a thought. The List of 500 is the jump start to the mind body crossover which transforms a thought or a desire into a reality. Take this assignment seriously, write down everything you want!

PSYCHOLOGICAL IMPRINTING

The real benefit of the List of 500 requires a full understanding of psychological imprinting. Science has discovered that psychological imprinting takes place in our minds as we focus on thoughts and objects and as we experience life through our senses. It is a mental learning process.

> Definition: In psychology and ethology, imprinting is any kind of phase-sensitive learning (learning occurring at a particular age or a particular life stage or a particular event) that is rapid and apparently independent of the consequences of behavior. Things become imprinted in our mind through different processes that utilize our different senses. i.e. sight, smell, touch, hearing, taste.

There is an interesting correlation/dilemma established between our conscious mind, our subconscious mind and the manifestation of our thoughts into realities, as it relates to imprinting. Philosophers, psychologists, scientists and psychiatrists have searched for years to determine where In the brain The Mind-Body Crossover takes place. There has been no definitive answer to date. The search and the debate continue.

There has been one interesting observation measured over the years by professionals in this field. They have not discovered where the cross-over between spiritual and physical occurs, but they have noticed one interesting correlation. It has been measured and observed that imprinting can be enhanced by implementing one simple technique. They found that writing down a thought, i.e. picking up a pen or a pencil and writing out a thought on a piece of paper, brings it to fruition faster than just thinking about a thought. This phenomenon was also observed if you typed the thought on a computer screen. It was noted that doing something physical, ink on paper, was the first manifestation of transforming a thought into something physical, i.e. Ink and paper. This discovery is at the cornerstone of The Mind-Body Crossover.

The process begins by setting aside at least two hours of your time, to make a list of 500 things you desire out of life. I recommend doing this during a weekend, where you are not pressed for time. Go to a favorite place where you can be alone and not interrupted. The list should include physical things and esoteric attributes you would like to acquire during your lifetime. Like a bucket list, but more expansive. i.e. the list should include the physical things, as well as the mental desires and esoteric thoughts and behaviors you would like to possess or acquire. I recommend taking a yellow legal notepad and physically write down your list with a pen or pencil. A computer or iPad could also be used to make your list. Your list could start with your "Bucket List" of major items.

Here are a few ideas to get started. You will soon run out of items and need to revert to more esoteric items as listed below:

1. new house
2. new car
3. trip to Africa
4. snow skiing in the Alps
5. summer home
6. Ferrari
7. an airplane
8. diamond ring
9. brushing your teeth every day
10. stop being a victim
11. flossing your teeth every day
12. stop swearing
13. saving an additional $100 a month for retirement
14. admit my faults
15. lose 40 pounds

16. fixing the broken cabinet in the bathroom
17. wash my car
18. stop drinking alcohol
19. learn how to play the piano
20. get my husband to read Five Love Languages
21. coach my sons little league
22. date night with my wife
23. date night with my kids
24. stop being passive aggressive
25. run a marathon
26. eat healthy foods
27. take vitamins every day
28. stop gossiping
29. stop watching I V
30. start watching more TV
31. buy flowers for my wife every month
32. paint the kids room
33. get Billy in a Montessori school
34. 100 sit ups every day
35. stop playing the victim
36. exercise four days a week
37. call my mom every week
38. stop looking at pornography
39. visit the zoo
40. stop lusting after other women
41. write a book
42. stop embellishing
43. write a poem
44. stop with the self-pity

45. stop smoking
46. build a film library of the family
47. pray every day
48. tell my husband I love him every day
49. call my sister
50. learn to speak Swahili
51. stop complaining
52. go to church every week
53. give to the poor
54. take a class on cooking
55. see a psychologist once a month
56. go on a retreat with my wife
57. go for a sleigh ride in Vermont
58. start a book club
59. climb Mount Everest
60. stop being a martyr
61. pray with my kids
62. plant a garden
63. get rid of credit card debts
64. plan a special vacation every year
65. stop cheating
66. stop insisting that I'm always right
67. stop pouting when I don't get my way
68. visit a relative
69. stop stealing
70. visit the sick
71. stop overeating
72. get involved with a charity
73. give to the downtrodden

74. learn to ask for help
75. learn to admit my faults
76. read a book a week
77. make a list of my resentments
78. stop lying
79. do something kind for one person a day
80. call an old friend every week
81. start a Bible study
82. buy a new suit
83. learn to wind surf
84. buy a tiny home
85. buy ten gifts for my wife on her birthday.
86. etc.

Go ahead and get creative with your list. I came up with these 85 items in a few minutes off the top of my head. I'm sure you can come up with a lot more. I suggest stopping if you make it to 500. In thirty years of speaking, I rarely meet someone who gets over 400. People who have taken my course still stop me in airports and tell me how many items they have on their List of 500.

Do not be concerned with how you state a desire when undertaking this assignment. It can be one word or ten. Complete or incomplete sentence. Just start with number one and keep filling up the pages. Don't worry about the list being in any order or fashion. You might want to keep it in a safe place for confidentiality, but other than that it can't be wrong, regardless of the content. Just list everything you have ever wanted or hope to have in your lifetime.

Once your list is complete, start categorizing the items by the area of life they represent for you. Most people use the seven listed below:

Financial - F

Career/Work - CW

Spiritual - S

Social/Personal Growth - SP

Intellect/Mind - M

Health/Physical - H

Family - F 1

This coded listing is immaterial and can be personalized to meet your needs. Most people agree that we have seven basic areas. Accuracy with these words/categories is not important to the process. Just put one of the codes next to each numbered item on your yellow pad. Once you have categorized each item, count how many you have in each category. This will tell you something more about your unique ability. If you are heavily overloaded in one area, you might consider that your focus needs to change. The object for your life is to be well balanced in all seven areas.

I learned a tremendous amount about myself when I finished my personal list of 500. FYI, I only got 237 items on my first attempt at this exercise. I remember putting my yellow notepad of the 237 items in a bottom drawer in my desk and forgot about them until inadvertently finding the list about five years later. I was amazed to read the list and found that I had accomplished over 65% of the things on this bucket list! It opened my eyes in a big way and was a major discovery and turning point helping me codify the mind-body crossover and revealing two very powerful secrets of successful goal setting.

CHAPTER SUMMARY

⚛ GOLDEN NUGGETS :

- Building a strategic plan for your life starts with making lists of desires and desired outcomes. i.e. The List of 500.

- Writing down a "thought", i.e. picking up a pen or a pencil and writing out a thought on a piece of paper brings it to fruition faster than just thinking about a thought. Much faster.

- Things are imprinted in our mind through different processes that utilize our different senses. i.e. sight, smell, touch, hearing, taste.

- A strategic plan for your life helps identify wants, needs and desires in all seven areas of your life.

- Your List of 500 should include physical things and esoteric attributes you would like to acquire during your life time.

- Hesitation kills!

ACTION ITEMS: (TELL ME WHAT TO DO)

- Set aside three hours to make your personal List of 500. Complete your list on a writing pad, iPad, computer, etc. Hand written is preferred but not mandatory.

- Categorize each item into one of the seven areas as previously noted.

CHAPTER EIGHT

GOALS AND MANTRAS

There are a million different ways to write and state goals. I'm a firm believer that goal statements should be stated as if the desired result has already occurred and leave the rest up to your subconscious mind which cannot determine realities. It will take you to fruition/manifestation if you put forth a vivid image, statement or dream. Remember, all humans are fear-based organisms, and we will procrastinate about almost anything out of fear of failure. Don't let fear keep you from writing out your goals and your goal statements. The main thing is to get something down on paper. You can always refine them later. Goal statements should be read daily to enhance the power of repetition. They should be formally reviewed and rewritten/ tweaked at least once a month and redone completely once a year. These review tasks, need to be listed on your monthly calendar into infinity! My business partner and spiritual mentor, Ty Sudds, wrote the following about fear and goal setting:

> When you give yourself options of why you can't accomplish your goals, then you begin to reason within yourself, to procrastinate your success and to "not" decide. But remember, you've already decided, when you decided not to decide, so technically you've made your decision, which is indecisiveness. Typically, excuses are nothing more than well planned lies. You're lying to

yourself and you're holding up your destiny and your purpose and disappointing those people who are awaiting your arrival!!! You can spend a lifetime studying, planning and orchestrating your dream, but the greatest gift of treatment for fear is getting started!!!! Copyright Ty Sudds 2014. All Rights Reserved.

The main point of this dissertation is that we are all looking for an easy way out. We are looking for the "get rich quick" process to success. There is no such thing! We must take responsibility to act. To start. To make a leap of faith! The process described in this book is only one of a multitude of ways. It's up to you to start the process. Create your pathway to success and use books and methods like ones described here, as an avenue/road map to get started. It takes great effort and massive action to build a strategic plan for your life, and there is no set way to do it.

In this chapter, we are focused on writing goal statements which help energize our subconscious mind. In a later chapter, we will learn how to write one major all-inclusive goal in each area of our life, that will become the standard bearer of our strategic plan. You will have seven major goals to give you purpose and focus.

Use your creativity to help develop your own style for your specific plan and use this book as a helpful tool to lead you along the way. When you write down your statements and review them daily, you effectively cross over the mind body barrier. Your subconscious mind will work overtime to ensure each statement becomes reality. Here are some examples to help you get started creating and writing your own goal statements to fit your desires and dreams.

EXAMPLES OF GOAL STATEMENTS

Health/Physical Goal: I am a person who is concerned about my body and always work to maintain my weight through proper exercise and diet. Only on occasion do I consume alcohol or high fat and cholesterol food. My body is my temple and I work to keep it that way.

> **NUGGET -** Note how this goal is stated as though you are already undertaking these healthy actions every day. You might still be overeating and never exercising, but don't tell your subconscious mind! If you truly want to change, make a commitment to start a new habit right now to become the person you are saying you are going to become. Tell your subconscious something positive, and it will help you obtain the desired outcome. Use this positive self-talk technique in all your personal goal statements. Emphasis added!

Social/Personal Growth: My peers respect me as I always try to properly evaluate and listen to both sides of every situation. All my decisions are made on a level which holds honesty and integrity as a top priority.

Financial Goal: I am a financially successful person. I am frugal with my money and set aside a portion of my earnings for retirement. I will be self-sufficient in my retirement due to good money management in my working career.

Spiritual Goal: I attend church on a regular basis and save a portion of every day to thank God for his goodness and kindness. I always find time to meditate and talk with God as I believe he is the creator and controller of the universe and will give me guidance in accomplishing my goals.

Social/Personal Growth: I am aware of the ravages of addiction and take personal responsibility to constantly monitor my behavior regarding the consumption of drugs, alcohol, pornography, over-eating, etc. My body and mind are my temples and I work tirelessly to keep them healthy, whole and free of abuse. Moderation and abstinence, where needed, are my secrets to success and a life filled with pure joy.

Social/Personal Growth: I am an outwardly positive person always. People always think of me as a "can-do" person because I always look for the good and positive in every situation and every person I meet. I smile a lot, knowing the value it brings to myself and others. I visualize myself as an upbeat person who is always positive and full of life.

Career/Work Goal: I am well respected by my partners and people I work with as I honestly work to protect their interest and position. I am genuinely concerned about their success and welfare and always portray this in my actions to them.

Social/Personal Growth: I am neat and orderly in everything I do. My work area is always kept free of clutter. I concentrate on being well prepared for all situations and take time every day to plan my activities. Being well organized is one of my best attributes. I am constantly planning and reviewing my goals as I know it is the only way to achieve.

Health/Physical Goal: I fully realize the importance of monitoring my health on a consistent basis. I schedule a thorough and complete medical physical exam every year and work closely with my caregivers to ensure my good health.

Spiritual Goal: I am a firm believer that my destiny is shaped by the quality of my personal relationships and I work to surround myself with quality people and never "fly with turkeys", only eagles. I work daily to expand my sphere of influence with people of high moral character.

Social/Personal Growth: I value my appearance and always work towards presenting a professional image. I am always aware that first impressions are vital to my success. I always introduce myself first with a firm handshake and good eye contact and dress appropriately for every situation.

Family Goal: I am recognized as a good father and mentor and always take time to spend time with my children. I am always aware of their needs and try always to think of them before myself in all situations. I work to have a private lunch with each of my children, one-on-one, at least once a month.

Health/Physical Goal: I am concerned with my mental health and realize the need and benefit of talking with a trained psychologist to help me grow to emotional maturity and get third party feedback. Evaluation of my desires, fears and my thought processes with the help of a trained psychologist is an intelligent thing to do on a consistent basis. I rarely go more than a month without a session on the couch.

Spiritual Goal: As a devoted Christian, I realize the importance of practicing my chosen religion. I set aside thirty minutes a day to read and memorize scripture.

Career/Work Goal: I am considered a leader at work and in the community and always work to help the less fortunate. I am concerned about my city and country and work to preserve our way of life. I pride myself on my leadership abilities and work to instill these characteristics of honesty and integrity in my employees and fellow man.

Social/Personal Growth: I am concerned about the less fortunate and always work to protect and help the poor and underprivileged. I reserve a portion of my time to help others and look for opportunities to be of service. I am always available to help the less fortunate.

Spiritual Goal: I take time every day to pray and meditate. I am a grateful person and take time every day to give thanks for all my many blessings. "Gratefulness is the great multiplier of all great things to come." I read scripture every day to seek God's guidance and will for my life and spend time reading and learning about meditation and how to quiet my "monkey" mind.

Financial Goal: I understand the compounding effect of saving money and deposit a minimum of $100 a month into a savings account in addition to my retirement/401K with the knowledge that it will grow to over a million dollars by the time I'm seventy-five years old. I will be self-sufficient in my retirement due to good money management in my working career.

Work/Career Goal: I consider myself an industry leader in my chosen profession and realize the need for continuing education. I always take at least two formal courses in my professional field every year. I set aside twenty minutes a day to read periodicals in my industry. I am aware that very few people read twenty minutes a day in their chosen profession and that this habit dictates I will become one of the foremost authorities in my chosen field, by practicing this discipline.

Social/Personal Growth: I am a persistent individual realizing the importance of always completing everything I start and working diligently to meet all deadlines, refusing to give up! I will persist until I succeed.

Spiritual Goal: I am a faith-filled practicing Christian, acknowledging that God blesses spiritually and financially all those that live 100% according to his precepts and commandments. I tithe a minimum of 10% and follow all his commandments to ensure a life filled with prosperity, spiritual fulfillment, peace and joy.

When you finish writing your own goal statements, you should have 7 X 7 = 49, I would suggest having at least seven goal statements for each of the seven areas of life. If you read these 49 goal statements every morning before you start work and rate yourself on your previous day's performance in relation to these goals, I can assure that your life will change immensely in less than a month. Your subconscious mind will do all the work! You will become the person! – Emphasis added!

POSITIVE AFFIRMATIONS, MANTRAS & GOAL STATEMENTS

The verbalization of positive affirmations, mantras and goal statements has been critical to reprogramming my mind for outstanding achievement. These are proven methods of self-improvement because of their capability to rewire our brains. Much like physical exercise, they raise the level of positive endorphins and push our brains to form new nerve centers of positive thoughts.

Repetition is paramount to implementation. So many of us focus only on negative self-talk, which is very detrimental to our psyche and needs to be avoided at all costs! However, positive statements, when internalized can help focus our subconscious on positive, instead of negative outcomes. By writing down mantras and goal statements (crossing the mind-body barrier), and hearing them often, I believe we can reprogram and rewire our brains and adjust our attitudes for the possibility of greatness.

Examples - Positive Affirmations and Mantras (Surf the net for additional mantras)

- I'm getting better every day in every way.
- Everything I need is coming to me.
- My life is blossoming in total maturity.
- I have everything I need to enjoy life.
- God is the master of my life.
- Perfect wisdom is in my heart.
- I love and appreciate myself just as I am.
- I accept all my feelings as part of me.
- I love to love and be loved.
- The more I love myself, the more love I must give to others.
- I now give and receive love openly.
- I am now attracting loving, satisfying relationships into my life.
- I am filled with creative power.
- Abundance-The light within me is creating miracles in my life here and now.
- I give thanks for my life of health, happiness and self-expression.
- This is my natural state of being. It's OK for me to have fun and enjoy myself and I do!
- I am worthy.
- I care about others.
- I choose only good for others.
- My heart is open to God.
- I am kind, generous and giving.
- I love and approve of myself.
- I make the right choices today and every day.
- I trust my intuition.
- Wonderful things unfold before me.
- I forgive myself for all the mistakes I have made.
- I trust myself to make great decisions.

- I am a better person from the hardship that I've experienced.
- I surround myself with people who treat me well.
- I choose to fully participate in life today.

Listening to positive affirmations and goal statements on audio tapes can improve your life in a positive way. There are numerous programs online that can assist you with the formation of excellent audio tapes. The internet has numerous sites on the "How To". I spend ten minutes every day, upon waking listening to positive affirmations and goal statements I wrote and recorded on my iPhone. Verbalization is key. When we speak our voices create a vibration an energy, that helps create The Mind-Body Crossover. Listen to or verbally repeat mantras and goal statements on a consistent basis for this energy to be created and The Mind-Body Crossover to be actualized. Very powerful.

MEDITATION, MIND CONTROL, FASTING & PRAYER

I can't stress enough the power of mind control, fasting, meditation, the subconscious mind and prayer. Fasting is foremost among these five disciplines. When starting a food fast you become more focused and free thinking. When free of carbohydrates and processed sugars, you start to think more clearly and it's much easier to reach a higher spiritual plane. There are great physical and mental benefits of fasting. Be sure to check with your physician before starting a fast. Years ago, I read a lot of material about mind control and found it very beneficial in setting my focus and manifesting my hopes, desires, and goals, not to mention the esoteric benefits of relaxation, peace and serenity received from meditation and mind control combined with fasting. I also read about the benefits of fasting and instruction on how to fast safely. I try to fast from all food at least one day a week with a two or three day fast once a quarter. When fasting, I drink a lot of water to help flush my entire system. Instead of a lengthy explanation about these processes, I encourage you to embrace these disciplines for an enlightening experience in mind control, meditation, fasting and prayer. Positive mind control can teach imagery techniques that many believe can rewire your subconscious mind by eliminating negative self-talk and negative programming and help tap into your true potential and achieve your goals.

Yoga can teach some valuable lessons about the powers of meditation and mind control. Learning to replace negative with positive self-talk and negative with positive habits is key to effecting permanent positive life change. Yogis (philosophers, who practice yoga and have achieved a high level of spiritual insight), have a term, samskara describing a mental process that occurs in our brains when we experience different emotions. Our life experiences, including our feelings, thoughts, words, actions and behaviors, all leave an impression on our consciousness. Every time we experience an emotional event our brain records the occurrence. Obsessive compulsive behaviors and addictions are examples of negative emotional events that can scar our psyche and create havoc in our lives. These negative and positive scars, or grooves in our brain, continue to grow and deepen as they are repeated in our consciousness. Neural pathways in our brain, as mentioned earlier, become larger and more dominant as you experience different emotions. Fortunately, the same process occurs with "positive" scars. These samskaras affect how we react and respond to the realities of life. Yoga can teach us how to reduce negative samskara and increase positive samskara. A very powerful life changing process.

Positive affirmations, mantras and goal statements are critical to helping learn to produce some very beneficial results in your life. I listen to a self-made, ten-minute audio tape, with meditative music in the background, of positive mantras every morning before I get out of bed. I also have an audio tape of my goal statements to listen to every morning before I arise. It has changed my life! When combining this audio meditation with fasting you will race towards an exhilarating spiritual experience. I also encourage learning the necessary relaxation exercises to see how to quickly reach a euphoric state of total relaxation in a short amount of time. (See below). This technique will help you quickly realize the benefit of fasting prior to meditation, mind control and prayer.

> Focus on this statement: Without fasting, prayer and meditation, I either think "too much" about myself or "too little" of myself!

Follow this procedure to produce a personal audio mantra tape recording:

- Start a recording on your iPhone or basic recorder, by playing relaxing music in the background. There are numerous sites on the internet where you can download background music for relaxation tapes and mind control.
- Once you find suitable background music, produce your own tape with approximately two minutes of relaxing music to help you relax and start the process. After recording two minutes of soft relaxing music, record the following words in soft, slow, diction at a relaxing pace:
1. "I am entering a state of deep relaxation, every time I hear the word relaxation, I go deeper and

deeper. I imagine the number three, the number three, the number three----which reminds me of deep relaxation."

2. "Whenever I hear the word relaxation, I go deeper and deeper into a total state of relaxation. I am imagining the number three, the number three, the number three, which reminds me of complete and total relaxation. I am relaxing my toes, my ankles and my calf muscles."

3. "I am relaxing my knees, my thighs and the bones inside my thighs. I am relaxing my pelvis and my chest. I am relaxing all my muscles, my tendons and all the cells and all the organs in my body."

4. "I am now focusing on relaxing my shoulders and my arms and my hands. I am focusing on relaxing the fingers on my hands."

5. "Relaxation. Relaxation."

6. "I am now focused on relaxing my throat and my face and all my facial muscles. I am relaxing my chin and my cheeks and my jaws."

7. "Relaxation. Relaxation."

8. "I am now focused on relaxing my ears, my forehead and my scalp. I am going deeper and deeper into a total state of total relaxation. Feeling a tingling sensation all over my body as I continue to relax and go deeper and deeper and deeper."

9. "I am now in a total state of total relaxation. I am now envisioning the number 2, the number 2 the number 2, as I am envisioning a quiet summer day on the beach with lots of sunshine and cool breezes. I am envisioning the number two, the number two, the number two.

10. "Relaxation, relaxation."

11. "I am continuing to be in a total state of relaxation. I am now entering level one, level one, level one."

As the relaxing music continues to play in the background, start reciting your mantras in a slow relaxed pace. Slowly repeating each mantra three times before starting the next mantra. You can include as many mantras as you like. I would suggest verbalizing the word "relaxation" several times after every three mantras as it helps you stay in a relaxed state conducive to energizing your subconscious mind.

Many of my mentees record all their goal statements and listen to them at least once a month. This can be a considerably longer tape as you should repeat each goal statement three times in a row to get the benefit of repetition. At the end, record the following: "I feel totally relaxed and rejuvenated. I can accomplish all things as my sub conscious mind is now prepared to help me manifest all my goals and desires. I feel totally relaxed and rejuvenated."

Here is how a typical relaxation exercise works:

- Find a quiet, comfortable place where you won't be disturbed.
- Turn off or lower the lights in the room.
- Get into a comfortable position either lying down or sitting.
- Close your eyes.
- Try relaxing your entire body all at once before you start.
- Breath slowly and deliberately, inhaling through your nose, exhaling through your mouth.
- Relax your body from your toes to the top of your head as you continue inhaling and exhaling.
- Focus relaxing for approximately two seconds on each part of your body.

- Move from your toes to the top of your head.
- Toes, feet, ankles, calves, knees, thighs, abdomen, chest, arms, hands, throat, facial muscles, ears and scalp (two seconds on each body part).
- Start your mantra tape and relax.

I highly recommend recording 3-5 different mantra/goal tapes of different lengths. I have a ten-minute tape I listen to every morning before I get out of bed and I have several longer tapes lasting 32 minutes and 49 minutes, I listen to these on weekends or when on an airplane or riding in a bus, car, etc.

FUTURE PACING

Future Pacing is a tool used to help imprint both positive and negative possibilities into our subconscious minds to help us grow and mature with an appropriate amount of hope and caution. It is a powerful tool to help us lead highly productive lives by altering our thoughts using creative visualization.

It is a process that serves two potential outcomes. One is to help codify our positive desires, dreams and goals. It's an attempt to step into the future (in our mind's eye) to visualize how great and satisfying our lives will be once we are successful in attaining our goals. It imprints positive pictures that show our subconscious mind where to focus.

The other use of Future Pacing is codifying potential negative outcomes of repeated destructive and negative behaviors. This helps us step into the future (in our mind's eye) to visualize what our lives will be like if we go back to old destructive negative habits/behaviors. It stimulates a fear reaction, interestingly used as a positive tool to help prevent negative consequences of relapses into addictive behaviors and other negative constructs. In this context, the process is used to codify our fears and negative outcomes if we engage in destructive activities involving addiction or other obsessive activities. It's a challenge to face the negative realities of falling back into bad behavior, addictions or crime as well as immature behaviors, i.e. passive aggressive behaviors, self-pity, blame, shame, etc. It causes us to react in a positive fashion driven by fear of negative consequences of returning to old negative behaviors. An example is whenever a drug addict or alcoholic is tempted to drink or use drugs and is fighting the "phenomena of craving". They immediately imagine the potential negative consequences and project themselves into the possible future of a bad hangover, going to jail, killing someone and going to prison, DUI, loss of family or death, etc. Future Pacing into these negative consequences is a helpful deterrent until the obsession to drink or use drugs has passed. Mastering this process activates an intense emotional response in the individual that can result in a lifesaving event. Once the craving has past you return to the positive side of Future Pacing by envisioning the benefits of being drug free, alcohol free etc.

CHAPTER SUMMARY

 ## GOLDEN NUGGETS:

- I'm a firm believer, that goals should be stated as if the desired result has already occurred and leave the rest up to your subconscious mind.

- Your subconscious mind cannot determine realities and will take you to fruition/manifestation if you put forth a vivid image, statement or a dream.

- Goals should be read daily to enhance the power of repetition.

- Write 7 goal statements in each of the seven areas of your life. Total = 49.

- If you read your 49 goal statements every morning before you start work, and rate yourself on your previous day's performance in relation to these statements, I can assure you your life will change immensely in less than 66 days.

- Mantras need to be verbalized. When we speak, our voices create a vibration, an energy, that helps bridge The Mind-Body Crossover.

- When we speak, our voices create a vibration, an energy, that helps create The Mind-Body Crossover. Listen to or verbally repeat these on a consistent basis for energy to be created and for The Mind-Body Crossover to be actualized. Listen to or repeat statements daily.

- There are great physical and mental benefits of fasting from food.

- Fasting - When you free yourself of carbohydrates and sugars, you start to think more clearly, and it's much easier to reach a higher spiritual plane, making it much easier to communicate with your subconscious mind.

- Learn the necessary relaxation techniques to quickly reach a euphoric state.

- Future Pacing is a tool used to help imprint both positive and negative possibilities into our subconscious minds to help us grow and mature with an appropriate amount of hope and caution.

- The other use of Future Pacing is codifying potential negative outcomes of repeated destructive and negative behaviors.

- Mastering this process activates an intense emotional response in the individual that can result in a lifesaving event.

- Hesitation kills!

ACTION ITEMS: (TELL ME WHAT TO DO)

- Try fasting from all food tomorrow after checking with your doctor.

- Create your personal list of goal statements and mantras. Write them out.

- Create your personal audio tapes.

- Set a reminder on your calendar to fast from food one day each week.

- Set a daily reminder on your calendar to listen to your mantra tape, and review goal statements and evaluate your performance.

CHAPTER NINE

THREE SECRETS OF HIGH ACHIEVEMENT

Triggers, Imprinting and The Countdown - The basic path to a life filled with freedom and joy! I spent a lot of my life looking for the answers to life. The three secrets shared in this chapter are very revealing and powerful if implemented in a sincere, consistent and dedicated way. They deal with repetition and habit formation. The two words (tools), Triggers and Imprinting, can help you switch your focus to a new type of behavior that ensures success. The Countdown gives you a phenomenal process that will change your life by teaching you how to take immediate and massive action to effect change. Together they will answer your request: TELL ME WHAT TO DO!

TRIGGERS - Secret #1

The first problem I always experienced with goal setting was my lack of commitment and follow-through. I would always have great enthusiasm for the process of writing goal statements but noticed that I soon became bored with the process. I never really changed my habits to ensure that my goal statements would manifest in my life on a consistent basis. Often, I would just plain forget about my goals, as they were never internalized into my consciousness. I had no good way to consistently remind myself of what I hoped to become because of my new stated goals. I would eventually go back to my old way of doing things, as I never established a new set of habits.

I've read on numerous occasions and in numerous publications that it takes a minimum of 66 days to form a new habit. That means it requires 66 days of consistently following a new behavior for it to become a part of my being or consciousness. Frustrated by lack of follow through, I gave a lot of thought to how I might solve this problem, once and for all. When I started studying the power of repetition, it convinced me of its' value and sparked a thought, that maybe I could use the same process to help codify my goal setting technique. How could I perpetually be reminded of my new goals moment by moment, day-by-day, all day, every day, for the rest of my life?

In my research, I noticed that we are all driven to certain thoughts or memories because of some sort of trigger or triggers. Certain words, pictures, sounds, smells, etc. remind us of certain things. I realized that I might be on to something that could assist me in the quest for goal achievement. What if I conditioned my mind to focus on a certain goal every time I was triggered by a certain word, event, smell, picture, etc.? I started to codify this concept by tying a specific event to a specific goal. For example, one of my general goals was "To persist until I succeed". The entire goal statement read as follows:

> I am a persistent individual. I realize the importance of always completing everything I start; work diligently to meet all deadlines and refuse to give up! I will persist until I succeed.

How could I internalize this desired goal to ensure I was reminded of it numerous times daily? I needed to link this statement to an "event" or "act" that I engaged in numerous times every day. What could I use as a trigger to remind me to "persist until I succeed"? The answer for me was "doors". How many doors do I open every day? A lot! Door to my car, office, shower, bedroom, cabinets, etc. I probably opened a door at least sixty or seventy times in a normal day. Many doors have closers or springs attached which require an effort to overcome some form of resistance. I use doors as a reminder to persist until I succeed. It takes effort to open a door, and I use this resistance to my advantage to ensure I always persist until I succeed at every undertaking. I set this trigger over twenty years ago and today it is impossible for me to open any door without being reminded to always persist until I succeed. Get the idea?

Today I have over twenty formal triggers that remind me of certain things I want to accomplish in my life. These triggers and associated desired behaviors have helped manifest some major positive changes in my life. They helped establish new habits through repetition and imprinting. I suggest you have a buck card (3" x 5" piece of paper) with a list of triggers and associated behaviors to help you memorize the association and corresponding trigger. An example of this process is what happens when you encountered an established trigger. Let's say you establish a trigger for an alarm to go off in your mind whenever you go over a speed bump in your car. This is a good example of something most of us encounter on a rather frequent basis. When you encounter a speed bump you say mentally to yourself: Slow down and focus on high value actions. This reminder will help keep you focused on something of value. It reminds you to live in a certain and productive way. Every time you encounter a speed bump this reminder will go off in your conscious and sub conscious mind, and it will begin to form a positive samskara in your brain. Review your buck cards daily until the associations become rote. Very powerful! These triggers will be very valuable when writing your strategic plan further explained later in this book.

Examples of triggers for your consideration:

> Every time I enter my shower and turn on the water I think of ….
>
> Every time I step into an elevator I think of ….
>
> Whenever I hear a horn honk I remember to….
>
> Whenever I smell….
>
> Whenever I see a….
>
> Whenever it starts to rain I…
>
> Whenever I get into my car…
>
> Whenever I touch….
>
> Whenever I taste….

Obviously, there are an infinite number of triggers that you can establish through memorization to help you achieve your goal statements. I recommend that you take an afternoon with a yellow pad and pencil to establish 15-20 formal triggers to coincide with your most critical goal statements. Write them down. Practice association of each word/sense with a desired goal statement for 66 days! It will quickly become a part of your psyche. Repetition as noted is the key to all great success. Creating triggers will help manifest desires quickly. I don't know of any better way to quickly establish a new way of thinking with instantaneous results as the combined use of triggers and imprinting!

IMPRINTING - Secret #2

The study of psychology has opened my mind to a lot of possibility thinking regarding goal setting. Along the way I have discovered a second powerful secret tied to the mind-body crossover. I have studied numerous approaches on the proper way to set goals and write goal statements, how you state goals, how you internalized them, what format you use, etc. A very revealing bit of information has come to light during my study about the power of writing down goals and goal statements, as opposed to just thinking about them. The overall result was mind-blowing. My research found that people who write down goals and goal statements, review them daily, and rewrite them monthly achieve considerably more than people who just think about their goals. I discovered that stating the goal as if it had already come to fruition was critical to overall goal achievement. If you are overweight at 200 pounds, instead of saying I want to lose seventy-five pounds, say "I'm a person who is concerned about my diet and recognize the health benefits of maintaining my desired weight of 125 pounds. I rarely eat high fat and cholesterol foods. My body is my temple and I work to keep it that way". Using this goal setting technique produces a much higher success rate, as the subconscious mind works toward the stated goal of 125 pounds, even while you are asleep. You are telling your subconscious mind that you already weigh 125 pounds.

Here is the SECRET. Limited research with my mentees found that participants who only think about goals and goal statements, without writing them down, achieve only 10 to 20%. Participants who write down goals in a positive fashion, read them daily and rewrite them monthly achieve between 60% and 70% of their goals. Wow!

When I realized this fact, I was blown away! That's a huge increase in success, just by writing them down in the correct fashion! What was going on? I'm convinced that the physical act of writing down a thought is in fact bridging The Mind-Body Crossover, as mentioned in Chapter 7. When this happens, even though we don't know where in the brain it occurs, we now know that taking a thought (spirit/mental) and materializing it on paper (physical) i.e. crossing the gap from the spirit realm to the physical realm, gives a much higher level of achievement! (i.e. ink on paper). There is a transfer of energy when we begin to write. With this knowledge, we would be remiss if we didn't start writing down all our goals and goal statements, rewriting all our goals, as if they had already occurred, and undertaking this assignment monthly. The physical act of writing is key as it energies and initializes The Mind-Body Crossover. Powerful secret!

THE COUNTDOWN 3,2,1,0-ACT! – Secret #3

"Embracing – DO IT NOW!"

I've been speaking for years on the power of change. If we want to get better, we must be able to change. Action is key to all change; however, change can be very scary! Action sounds like a simple concept but, unfortunately, we are programmed mentally and physiologically not to act. We possess the desire and have the knowledge to change, but don't have a good system to act on this desire and knowledge. As a matter of fact, our brains have a protection mechanism that steers us away from acting. Whenever a thought, especially a new thought, occurs consciously, our brains scream: "Hold on, check this out, don't act to quickly, this is new territory, it might be dangerous!" In that split second, we usually hesitate, rethink and re-position.

That very short moment of hesitation is the culprit! Here comes Secret #3!

Hesitation will kill your dreams. Hesitation will prevent you from changing. Hesitation is a very destructive habit and one very difficult to break. When hesitation strikes, I train mentees to ACT immediately. When you have a creative thought, you need to act on it immediately before your brain convinces you to do otherwise. You only have a few seconds to act, 3.7 seconds to be more exact. I like to use a countdown theory of counting backwards from three to zero and force myself to act before I get to zero.

There is a fine line between success and failure. Life is made up of "small" bad decisions and "small" good decisions. Every decision we make can totally change our entire life. Emphasis added! Let me repeat: *EVERY DECISION WE MAKE CAN TOTALLY CHANGE OUR ENTIRE LIFE!!*

Addiction shows how The Countdown can be used to prevent catastrophic events from occurring when a small bad decision point is facing an addict. When new in recovery, an addict often becomes obsessed with the urge to have a drink or to use drugs. It is often a life or death situation with only a few seconds to react. When the urge to drink or "use" manifests in the brain of the addict, he has only 3.7 seconds to react by Future Pacing as outlined earlier. i.e. (recalling the possible negative outcomes of taking the drink), such as hangover, jail, killing, going to prison for DUI, loss of family, death, etc. He can further increase his chances of beating the urge by calling his psychologist or mentor immediately to discuss the problem and get personal help. When the urge appears, he Future Paces immediately and starts The Countdown – 3, 2, 1, 0-ACT. His goal is to call his support system before he gets to ACT. Repetition of this rote exercise helps him make a "small" good decision that could save his life. It scrambles his brain and moves the incident immediately to his prefrontal cortex. A very helpful tool. Remember that hesitation kills!

Unfortunately, our brains try to keep us from making any quick, new or creative decisions. Training yourself to act quickly and decisively with the right decisions is the key to success. It requires action, immediate action. Research tells us that we must break the cycle of "habit loops" to effect real change. "Habit loops" (much like samskara, mentioned earlier) are hidden deep in our subconscious mind, and we react to them repeatedly without being aware they even exist. They produce rote action coming from deep in our brains. Science tells us that these habit loops must be interrupted or scrambled to learn new data and create new possibilities. Your prefrontal cortex is the part of your brain used when taking new action, doing something difficult or creative, like goal setting or strategic thinking/planning. It takes a lot of energy to get the ball rolling. The prefrontal cortex is used to effect change. Being able to act immediately, within several seconds, is the first step in breaking negative, established habit loops whenever one of these thoughts enters our mind. This occurs in your prefrontal cortex. It is imperative to interrupt/scramble these negative thoughts the moment they come into your mind.

The same process works for a good, creative thought. If conditioned to take immediate action when you have a creative thought, you can start to build positive habit loops which can help you realize your dreams. This new habit of consistently breaking old negative, firmly established habit loops and substituting healthy, positive ones will allow you to incorporate positive change in every area of your life. 3,2,1,0-ACT!

A good example of a destructive habit loop is the tendency to hit reset on your alarm clock in the morning. Many psychologists suggest using a scrambling method to help break these habits substituting a positive habit loop in its place. Mel Robbins in her bestselling book, The Five Second Rule, uses the analogy of getting out of bed like a rocket ship after she counts down from five to one, every morning when she hears the alarm. I encourage you to read her book for a complete explanation of the technique and science behind the need to act immediately to effect change. I've been encouraging many of my older mentees to use a similar concept involving stretching upon awakening. I call this technique "Stretching for Success". I've personally been a slow riser and have trouble jumping out of bed when my alarm goes off. It's easier for me to take baby steps, but I do take immediate action to ensure I scramble my rote habit of hitting the snooze. When my alarm goes off, I start the mental countdown in my brain slowly and deliberately verbalizing: 3,2,1,0-ACT. When I get to the word ACT in The Countdown, which usually takes a couple of seconds, I start a new habit of reaching over immediately and turning off the alarm instead of hitting the snooze button. Immediately I start a new behavior of counting backwards from 100 to zero, at a brisk pace while I start stretching every muscle in my entire body for a full minute while lying in bed. While still lying in bed, I wiggle, flex and stretch each muscle group for about one minute. I gradually become more awake and focused on my counting. Remember, counting is action. Action promotes more action. Action scrambles your thought process and activates your prefrontal cortex. At the end of the stretching exercise I start/focus on another desired new habit like, exercising, praying or meditating and I start with The Countdown, 3,2,1,0-ACT! When I get to ACT, I immediately jump out of bed and start an exercise program, or my prayer ritual, or my meditation ritual. My "Rise and Shine" program outlined below fully explains my morning ritual that is ignited with The Countdown.

This method can be used to break any negative habit loops hidden deep in your brain. This process interrupts your habitual inner brain thoughts and brings your new habit loop into your prefrontal cortex. You must establish this new mental rule of acting immediately, within several seconds, to effect change. Emphasis added. You only have a few seconds to scramble, 3,2,1,0-ACT! Taking immediate action is the key to this process. It is very similar to the Mind-Body Crossover where the secret to success is picking up a pen and starting to write. The action of writing converts a mental thought into a physical manifestation of ink on paper, i.e. the secret of crossing over the barrier. In this action scenario, counting backwards from 100 to 0 is the key. In its simplest configuration, counting is a form of acting that scrambles your old rote long-term behavior. Counting backwards requires focus and immediately scrambles our rote way of thinking forcing a new possibility of establishing a new positive habit loop. Very powerful! It's the single most powerful tool I've discovered to make permanent, lasting change in my life. I've labeled it "The Countdown"! Apply this technique in all seven areas of your life. The moment you encounter any "situational hesitation" or "negative thought pattern", you must wake up your prefrontal cortex by starting The Countdown 3,2,1,0-ACT! with a focus on your new desired outcome (habit) instead of your old rote habit. Focusing on the new thought is all you must do to break the rote habit, and you do this with The Countdown 3,2,1,0-ACT!!

Another example is when you catch yourself daydreaming about the past or the future. Daydreaming about the past is usually depressing. Daydreaming about the future usually produces anxiety. You want to be living in the present! I call this making a conscious effort to give up "fantasy" thinking. (Wishing/hoping I was wealthy or skinny or popular, etc.) Wishing and hoping without acting to change, is a lie and very destructive to your mental health and is not centered. Hope is not a strategy! You must take 100% responsibility for controlling your thoughts and making efforts to delete bad thinking behaviors by taking new, positive and immediate action.

Whenever catching yourself daydreaming, stop and focus on the present! Instead of daydreaming, focus on something positive like all the things you should be grateful for in your life. Focus on the things you can do to become wealthy, skinny, popular, etc. instead of wishing and hoping that they will miraculously be given to you without merit. Gratefulness is the language of love. God is love.

Take immediate action on every positive and negative thought that enters your mind. Do it now, before your brain convinces you otherwise! Pick up the phone, write the email, start the diet, confront your boss, talk to your husband, talk to your wife, -- take the first step immediately! You will be amazed at how quickly The Countdown will change your whole life. Start today. 3,2,1,0-ACT! The more you practice this behavior, the quicker you change.

When making a conscious decision to change, your brain knows something new is getting ready to take place and goes into defense mode. It wants you to stay in the safe confines of your inner brain. You must interrupt or scramble this rote process with The Countdown, all day, every day until a new habit loop is established. You need to act quickly and implement your new thought(s) before your brain goes into protection mode of doing nothing or procrastinating to infinitum. As mentioned earlier, "hesitation" is a goal killer! As you continue to repeat this new way of acting when encountering old habits, you become stronger and stronger at combating the culprit, the killer. As discussed earlier, it takes repetition. You can't think your way into change, you must act. You can never change the things that trigger you, but you can establish new triggers that will form new samskara that will change your life and help you obtain your dreams. This repetitious action will manifest itself into lasting behavior change.

Starting a strategic plan for your life and setting goals are good examples of taking control of your life immediately. It's imperative that you act immediately and start implementing this new positive creative thought. The moment you feel "hesitation" you must wake up your prefrontal cortex with The Countdown! Act. Don't procrastinate. Start right away. Start NOW! 3,2,1,0-ACT!

CHAPTER SUMMARY

♣ GOLDEN NUGGETS:

- Triggers and Imprinting - These secrets deal with repetition and habit formation.

- It takes a minimum 66 days to form a new habit. You must consistently follow a new behavior for it to become a part your being/consciousness.

- The power of repetition and word association are the secrets behind triggers and imprinting.

- Certain words, pictures, smells, etc. all remind us of certain things. (Triggers)

- What if I conditioned my mind, to focus on a certain goal every time I'm triggered by a certain word, event, smell, picture, etc. – A Secret.

- Practice association of each word/sense with a desired goal for 66 days.

- My research found that people who write down goals, review them daily, and rewrite them monthly achieve considerably more than people, who just think about their goals. 70% vs. 20%!

- The physical act of writing, ink on paper, is key as it energies and initializes The Mind-Body Crossover. Powerful secret!

- Planning is the key to all success, followed by massive action.

- Hesitation will kill your dreams. Hesitation will prevent you from changing.

- Hesitation is a very destructive habit and one that is very difficult to break.

- Emphasis added. Let me repeat: EVERY DECISION WE MAKE CAN TOTALLY CHANGE OUR ENTIRE LIFE

- "Habit Loops" are much like samskara, mentioned earlier. Habit loops are hidden deep in our subconscious mind and we react to them repeatedly without being aware they even exist.

- The moment you encounter any "situational hesitation" you must wake up your prefrontal cortex and start The Countdown 3,2,1,0-ACT!

- To change, you must interrupt this sequence by forcing your new thought into your prefrontal cortex. You accomplish this with The Countdown. 3,2,1,0-ACT!

ACTION ITEMS: (TELL ME WHAT TO DO)

- Make a list of 15-20 possible triggers for future use in your strategic plan. These are things that you see, do or observe numerous times a day.

- When your alarm goes off every morning, Start The Countdown, instead of hitting the snooze button – for the remainder of your life. Every morning!

- Whenever you catch yourself daydreaming, stop and focus on the present!

- Take immediate action on every positive thought that enters your mind and every negative thought. Do it now, before your brain convinces you otherwise!

- The moment you feel "hesitation" you must wake up your prefrontal cortex with The Countdown! Act. Don't procrastinate. Start right away. Start NOW! 3,2,1,0-ACT!

CHAPTER TEN

STRATEGIC PLANNING

In 1979, I joined The Horne Company Realtors in Houston, one of the largest commercial real estate firms in the city. I landed a job in their property management department and got my first look at how a highly successful, mid-level company operated. Getting an opportunity to work at The Horne Company was no easy task. I had to navigate eight intense interviews before I was hired. This stringent interviewing was one of the first important lessons I learned on how to run a great company. Making good hiring decisions is one of the major, if not the most important key to success, in assuring you have a high-performance company. This lengthy interview concept, taught me a lot about the hiring process and was later incorporated into my training and consulting business.

The formal "strategic planning process" was just starting to catch on for smaller mid-sized companies in the early seventies. Previously, Strategic Planning was reserved for the larger more sophisticated Fortune 500 companies. Today, it has grown to a very sophisticated level, and some fortune 500 companies are spending millions of dollars in the strategic planning area on an annual basis. The differences between business and personal are subtle yet transformative.

Corporations focus on three areas when producing a strategic plan - Profit, Growth and Image. They are concerned with only these three areas. Each contains important ingredients and all three are focused on building shareholder value, which is the only true reason for the existence of a business corporation. Building a strategic plan for life is similar in many ways. Both work under the same format of setting goals and placing deadlines on completion. The important key here is setting the deadlines! This forces you to act to meet the deadline. This is the secret to all success - Acting! Taking Massive Action!

PERSONAL MISSION STATEMENT

In Chapter Five we learned how to write a statement describing our unique ability. It is the first step in building a good strategic plan for your life. The second step is writing your personal mission statement. A personal mission statement provides clarity and gives you a sense of purpose. It defines who you are and how you will live. It is the foundation of how you will live your life in the future and gives direction. Hopefully it will become the guiding force in your life. It demands a lot of thought and consideration. Following are several steps to help you codify your thoughts to create a meaningful personal mission statement:

1. Review mission statements of individuals that you emulate. (Google)
2. List the qualities you admire most in others. Mental, physical, emotional, spiritual.
3. Define the kind of person you want to become. Think about your legacy. Future pace.
4. Identify your core values and your integrity absolutes.
5. List the outcomes you want to achieve. Future pace to the end of your life and look back.
6. Ensure your personal mission statement reflects the abilities outlined in your unique ability statement.

7. Craft your statement. Re-craft your statement until you are satisfied.

Keep it simple, clear and relatively short. It can be a few sentences to a couple of paragraphs. You can write it as a statement that flows or with bullet points. You want a statement that will guide you in your day to day actions and decisions. Keep your long-term goals in mind as you construct the statement. Keep it positive. Focus on what you want rather than what you don't want.

My Personal Mission Statement:

"To be a giver and positive influence as a mentor to all I encounter. To continually search for and experience a life filled with absolute joy while enjoying healthy choices and habits. To be a humble, honest, energetic participant in all things I attempt with a focus on integrity in all I do. Being a can-do, inquisitive personality with a passion for living life to its fullest while helping others, focused on living in the moment. God conscious all day every day." - Gary Dahse

THE STRATEGIC PROCESS

Below is a depiction of the format and flow of a Strategic Plan for a Business:

Goals (3) – Profit, Growth, Image

Objectives – one or two objectives for each goal

    Strategies – three or four strategies for each objective

        Tactics – 3-100+ for each strategy

            Timeline – time frame (date) to complete each item

                Accountability – person or group responsible

In constructing the strategic plan for life, your thought process should keep in mind a similar structure with subtle differences explained below. Follow this format for the accomplishment of goals and desires in all seven areas of your life. There can be considerable overlap, but the premise is the same. Refer to the listing of the potential seven areas of your life that need to be included in a Strategic Plan for Your Life. I previously mentioned the process of how to write goal statements and the importance of structure to ensure achievement of each goal statement. Once your conscious mind is fed the basics of your desires, the subconscious mind will work to achieve them in your life even while you sleep!

I recommend that in addition to writing 49 short goal statements you also write one major summary goal for each area of your life. All major goals should include a deadline for completion and follow the steps outlined below. You can have "long term goals" as well as "short term goals" in addition to your original 49 goal statements. These seven major goals represent most of your strategic plan for your life. Take time to be thorough. Follow this format as closely as possible:

- Name the goal.
- Name the rewards of obtaining the goal-i.e. the feeling you will have.
- Name the obstacles to obtaining the goal.
- Name the knowledge/education needed to accomplish the goal.
- Name the action items (steps) needed to accomplish the goal.
- Name the date of completion.

Review, rewrite and monitor progress for these seven major goals every month. Writing is key to the process. (i.e. imprinting).

Over the last forty years I have collected a lot of success tips to help me live a more joyful, productive life. I have incorporated them into my strategic plan for life. Many tips are simple but have given me major advantages to get ahead and enjoy life with more gusto and passion. If you are interested in achieving all the things outlined in the book's first paragraph, implementing the ideas below will help jump start the process. I teach many of these skills in my consulting business and more detail is available on my website listed at the back of this book. I have outlined some of the more helpful tips below. Incorporate them into your strategic plan.

Following are additional suggestions and concepts for consideration in developing and implementing your personal strategic plan:

- o 1) RISE AND SHINE
- o 2) YOUR CALENDAR CONTROLS YOUR LIFE
- o 3) WORKPLACE POLITICS
- o 4) RELATIONSHIPS AND MARRIAGE
- o 5) TOASTMASTERS
- o 6) SERVICE ORGANIZATIONS–GIVING BACK
- o 7) CAREER-INDUSTRY ASSOCIATIONS
- o 8) AN ETERNAL, FOCUSED LEARNER
- o 9) BUCK CARDS
- o 10) JOURNALING
- o 11) PICTURE BOARDING
- o 12) Notebook

RISE AND SHINE

You must have personal reflection time to escalate personal growth and maturity as it's a critical element of building and maintaining a strategic plan. I believe the best time for this undertaking is early in the morning before the day dawns. I require mentees to start getting up an hour earlier every morning for exercise, meditation, prayer, daily review and quiet time. If you are a person that needs a certain amount of sleep to function, I recommend going to bed an hour earlier to allow for one hour of uninterrupted reflection time, in the morning. When your alarm goes off, start your ritual, and follow it religiously. I personally have broken my wake-up ritual into six segments before I hit the shower:

1. 1-3 Minutes - Intense stretching exercises while I am lying in bed.

2. 10 Minutes - Physical exercise, isometrics, running in place, pushups, etc. Research indicates that 10 minutes of increased heart beat and sweating produces serotonin and endorphins, providing a healthy chemical boost and raising our positive emotional level exponentially, the best way to start any day.

3. 10 Minutes - Prayer ritual - On my knees. Thanking God for all blessings, praying for others, praying for guidance and praying for self.

4. 20 Minutes-Audio meditation tape – Mantras, goal statements, affirmations.

5. 10 Minutes - Listen to recording of Psalms 1, 85, 91, Isaiah 61, Proverbs 3 and 31 in the Christian Bible.

6. 10 Minutes - Random motivational readings: spiritual, self-help, religious, inspirational, etc.

Performing this ritual as a high-value activity reinforces your commitment to yourself and your strategic plan. I recommend this activity for the morning as you are more rested physically and mentally. Emphasis added, every morning!

YOUR CALENDAR CONTROLS YOUR LIFE

Planning is the key to all success in constructing your strategic process, followed by massive action. It is imperative that you let your calendar control your life. It's the key factor in any strategic process because it enforces and drives action. With today's technology, this is a simple solution to an age-old problem of forgetting what we are supposed to do next. Setting recurring reminders and alarms is simple with today's iPhone. We can't act if we don't know what we are supposed to do next and when to do it. All good strategic plans have deadlines for completion of each goal or task. I encourage you to set a phone alarm for every deadline outlined on your strategic plan! It's advisable to take several hours at the beginning of the year to set all annual reminders that are part of your plan - birthdays, anniversaries, vacations, standing meetings that occur daily, weekly, monthly, quarterly and annually. Pay special attention to the items you know you should do but are hesitant to put on the calendar because you have a weak constitution. An example might be attending church on a weekly basis. You might not want to put it on your calendar because you like to sleep in on Sundays or play bridge or golf instead. By putting it on your calendar, church will slowly start to preempt sleep, bridge or golf as subconsciously, you know your personal growth and maturity will benefit more by attending Church. A great way to help establish a new healthy habit and a new high-value activity.

WORKPLACE POLITICS

If you work in corporate America, no strategic plan for your life can be complete without addressing and understanding the psychology of the workplace. Most people spend about half of their lives either working for themselves or for someone else. Having a plan that addresses the nuances of this part of your life is critical for success. Read as many books and articles on this subject as you can find.

This conversation needs to begin at the top of the corporate ladder, to fully understand the psychology of the workplace and the dysfunction of most corporate entities. This discussion recalls for me a cesspool of words, descriptions, and phrases – abuse of power, arrogant prestige, backstabbing, lying, gossip, manipulation, emotional immaturity, malicious intent, vindictive behavior, authoritarian behavior, hateful intent, sexual harassment, anger, passive aggressive behavior, argumentative nature, unequal treatment, chauvinism, staunch feminist agenda, favoritism, intimidation… the list goes on and on. Unfortunately, my opinion of most businesses dictates there is an overabundance of these traits being displayed at every level of many companies. I am often hired to help mitigate consternation between employees in middle management positions in companies. A much bigger problem usually exists in upper management, in the "C Suites", i.e. the CEO, COO, CFO, CIO, etc. I have been hired on several occasions to help mitigate consternation in the "C Suites" of some high functioning business entities. I'm always amazed at the maturity level of the upper executives, or should I say the lack of maturity. I find that many CEO's suffer from a very real fear that the world will find out that they are imposters! Not all, but many.

I'm convinced that rising to the level of one's incompetency is considered a must to land a "C Suite" position at many companies. Unfortunately, many executives rise through the corporate ranks with a very low level of emotional awareness, much less any real emotional maturity. They often gain these "C Suite" positions due to their aggressive behavior styles and personality faults outlined in the cesspool of words listed above. This is a result of being fear based. As an employee in one of these types of companies, you need to be aware of this dysfunction, and be careful of your behavior. Life is not "fair" in these types of companies. Never trust anyone in this type of organization! If you are in a "C Suite" position, you need to ask yourself if you are guilty of any of the behaviors listed above. If you are guilty, find a psychologist to help you overcome these character flaws. This is hard work, but it will give you a lot of peace and your career will skyrocket once you master emotional maturity.

Fortunately, not all companies are this way. Exceptionally well-run companies usually hire, or have on staff, industrial psychologists. They help key employees with people management responsibilities, learning how to deal with difficult situations and emotionally immature people. They also encourage mentoring inside their organization. If you don't have at least three trusted mentors, get to work on finding them immediately. I teach this skill later in this book.

Never assume your boss knows what he is doing! Always act as though he does!! Read material on leadership and management if you want to get ahead. <u>Never send out a fiery email without sitting on it for twenty-four hours.</u> Practice the art of intentional listening. Volunteer for the tough assignments. Never make your boss look bad. Never gripe or complain without giving a suggestion on how to make it better. Ask smart questions. Shut up, listen and repeat. Never "bad mouth" anyone and never, never, ever gossip (with anyone, anywhere)! Never go into an interview without anticipating the top ten questions and the appropriate answer to each that will be asked in the interview. Research the company and the industry in detail before the interview. Be up on current events, always dress appropriately and meet and greet with a firm handshake and relaxed, direct eye contact. Always have a professional writer critique and design your resume and bring extra copies to the interview. Once you get a job, be honest, ethical and moral, and you will eventually reach the top. Remember that great companies always pay for performance, leadership and value. Bring all three if you really want to succeed.

RELATIONSHIPS AND MARRIAGE

As a victim of divorce, I'm not one to give advice. However, my life journey has allowed me to observe some successful marriages and some successful relationships. I have seen some of the tools others have used to avoid relationship problems now and, in the future, to live healthy, productive, sharing and caring lives filled with intimacy and hope.

Recently, I've read two books that have changed my perspective and attitude immensely about the need to fully understand the opposite sex to have a healthy, sustainable and exhilarating relationship. Men and women are wired differently and until you understand the intricacies of these differences, I believe it's almost impossible to survive and sustain a healthy relationship with the opposite sex. My personal advice, is to never get married until you have dated for two years, three might even be better. Most marriage counselors will tell you that the "in love" stage lasts eighteen months and you can't think clearly during this stage! To fully and completely understand your significant other, to truthfully understand if you are a good fit for each other, you must be out of the "in love" stage. Here are four books I highly recommend if you are in a serious relationship or considering marriage:

"Sacred Marriage" by Gary Thomas

"The Five Love Languages" by Gary Chapman

"Nine Must Have Conversations for a Doubt Free Wedding Day" by Gary Thomas

"Cherish" by Gary Thomas

TOASTMASTERS

It makes no difference if you are an introvert or an extrovert, everyone loves a great speaker, and most everyone emulates and respects even mediocre speakers because of their own personal fears related to public speaking. Many introverts have a huge aversion to public speaking and feel uncomfortable getting up to speak in front of a crowd. Some extroverts also have a fear of public speaking. Toastmasters is an organization that trains individuals to overcome the fear of public speaking and gives them tools to face their fears and polish their skills. Being able to speak in front of others is a tool that will provide a huge advantage in the marketplace. I encourage you to join Toastmasters regardless of your fear. Every good personal strategic plan should include learning to become proficient at this skill. Feel the fear and do it anyway!

SERVICE ORGANIZATIONS – GIVING BACK

The Exchange Club of the Magic Circle was a Godsend to my business career and my ongoing quest to strive for personal spiritual maturity. The Exchange Club is a national service organization that taught me the benefits and value of giving back to my fellow man and my community. Prior to my thirtieth birthday, I was a total taker! Take, take, take! Today I think of myself as a giver due to my experience of joining service organizations. I recommend all my mentees join a service organization and get them on the "Free Lunch" Program to ascertain the best fit for their individual personalities. Giving back to your community will do wonders for your business career in addition to doing something good for others. Most of my long-term business relationship were generated through joining service organizations dedicated to helping the less fortunate. It is also a great source for job opportunities and building career enhancing relationships. I would venture to guess that 90% + of all highly successful entrepreneurs belong to a service organization.

Here is how the "Free Lunch" Program works. All service organizations, like Exchange Clubs, Kiwanis Clubs, Rotary Clubs, Lions Clubs, etc., are constantly looking for new members and they have standing invitations to anyone looking to join. Most clubs meet weekly for breakfast, lunch or dinner. They usually have a guest speaker and last approximately one hour. In Houston, there are over 6,000 different service organizations in the five-county greater MSA. Just about every hotel in every major metropolitan area in the country hosts numerous different service organizations every day. All you need do is walk down the private dining wing of any hotel at meal time, and you will probably find several organizations holding their weekly meeting. If you inquire at the door they will almost always ask you to join them for a free meal as their guest. I get my mentees to visit 20-30 different clubs until they find an organization they like. This is a target rich environment for up-and-coming entrepreneurs looking to establish business relationships and career opportunities. A must consideration for any person looking to jump start their lives and their careers!

I have been involved with several organizations in my career - The Exchange Club, The ESCAPE Center for Abused Children, The Brookwood Community and Bridges to Life Prison Ministry. All have been extremely rewarding from a personal fulfillment standpoint. I also have helped/benefited financially some very worthwhile organizations. As President of the Exchange Club of the Magic Circle in 1985-86, I worked with two individuals who were some of the biggest "Givers" I've ever met. Gerald Franklin, a highly successful entrepreneur and former National President of the Exchange Clubs of America and Ray Daugbjerg, former Honorary Consul General of Denmark. These were two of the most selfless people I've ever worked with, who taught me a lot about altruism. During my tenure as President of the Exchange Club, Ray started the Houston Golf Marathon fund raiser, for our local Exchange Club that to-date has raised over $15,200,000 for The Brookwood Community (a God-centered educational, residential and entrepreneurial community for adults with functional disabilities). I only had a small part in this undertaking as the president of the club, but it shows the power of being involved with service organizations that exist to give back to their community. Gerald Franklin on the other hand has spent a major part of his life helping grow and expand the Escape Family Resource Center for the prevention of child abuse, in addition to numerous other charitable organizations. These two close friends have benefited me personally and professionally over the years and taught me the true meaning and value of giving without expectation of reward. Thanks, Ray! Thanks, Gerald!

If you truly want to be a leader and winner, get involved with a good service organization and give back to your community! No life is complete without service. Make this a major part of your strategic plan.

CAREER-INDUSTRY ASSOCIATIONS

Highly successful entrepreneurs are usually heavily involved with shaping their respective industries. If you are an accountant, you should be a member of your industry association that supports accountants. I believe this is the National Society of Accountants (NSA). If you are a property manager or own a property management company you should be a member of the Institute of Property Management (IREM) or possibly The Building Managers and Owners Association (BOMA), etc. Regardless of your profession, doctor, lawyer or Indian Chief, involvement in your career industry association is a must for the budding entrepreneur or high performer. In my opinion, your goal should be to eventually become the leader/President of the organization. This involvement will jump start your career.

AN ETERNAL, FOCUSED LEARNER

Most of us are addicted to distraction. We are slaves to social media, our emails, the weather, the news, gossip, phone calls, etc. We spend an inordinate amount of time on unproductive distractions when we could be growing and learning. I call these distractions the "minor" things preventing us from acquiring legendary greatness. They are energy vampires sucking us dry and preventing us from achieving our dreams. You can be distracted, or you can be legendary, but you can't be both. The secret to genius is focus. Stop distractions.

Here are two new, one-hour, daily habits for your consideration if you want to achieve legendary greatness and become the person you want to be. Do something epic!

First Habit: Start every work day disconnected from social media and your phone and emails and focus on the one thing that will bring you closer to your major impact goal. Focus on it intently every day for one hour before you start your daily work routine. Personal mastery demands ample quiet time. No distractions. Just focus.

Second Habit: Spend one hour every day of your life learning something new. Never go to sleep without confirmation that you spent at least 60 minutes learning something new. The best way to accomplish this is books-on-tape. Listen on the way to work every day. Stop listening to depressing news and do something valuable. Learn a new language. Learn a new skill. Audio tapes in your car. My friends call this Rush Hour College. Become an eternal learner!

BUCK CARDS

The buck card is my personal best tool that utilizes this secret for achievement, and it's so easy to implement. Forty years ago, before personal computers, I carried buck cards to take notes. A buck card is a 3-inch by 5-inch index card made of heavy stock that will fit in your shirt pocket. Today, most people use their phone or iPad to take notes, but I still recommend using physical buck cards for this goal setting technique as it will help you bridge The Mind-Body Crossover. (ink on paper). Rarely will you see me without a buck card in my pocket or in my car on the console. On the front of the card, I have ten major things that I want to focus on for the entire upcoming year. On the back, I have five listings of my major bucket list items for the upcoming year. When riding in my car, I review my lists at stop lights and in heavy traffic. Each item might be only one or two words - eat healthy, pray daily, fast one day a week, review goals daily, be positive, date night with spouse, smile more, compliment more, exercise every day, private time with kids daily, see my shrink twice a week, etc. On the back of the card I try to list "Major Impact" goals. These are bucket list items dealing with Joy, instead of Happiness goals, as I will further define later in this book. Instead of listing something like going on an African Safari, a happiness goal which obviously might be a lot of fun, a much more beneficial goal would be going on a Couples Retreat to solidify my marriage relationship! Another goal might be to attend a spiritual retreat to learn more about meditation or prayer rituals. Another goal might be to have a private date night with each of my children once a month – just the two of us. This simple card has been responsible for helping me more than anything else due to its repetition and imprinting capability. (ink on paper). I use buck cards to remind me of many things and sometimes use them to take general notes when not by my computer. I also use them to write personal notes to friends and employees. However, I only allow myself one "master" buck card a year for the ten goals, and I work to establish a "trigger" for each item on the list. By the end of the year, it is worn and tattered with smudges, dirt, coffee stains, etc. Allowing only one card per year trains your subconscious mind to highly value the card. Carry it with you every day and review 5 or 6 times a day. You will be amazed at your level of accomplishment and new habit generation because of the repetition and imprinting - (ink on paper). This needs to become one of your high-value activities.

JOURNALING

Journaling breeds clarity. It helps your inner person change your outer person. It helps you find your passion when undertaken as a daily habit. It is a great way to express gratitude, the key to dealing with emotions and living a life filled with joy. Society says we should suppress feelings which is very bad as it causes us to bottle up fears and anxieties. Journaling helps you to release these poisons and frees you to be humble and grateful, the key to living a life filled with passion. I recommend my mentees start every morning's journaling exercise with a list of ten things they are grateful for today.

Imprinting takes place when we pick up a pen or pencil and start to write. This is the simplest form of bridging The Mind-Body Crossover - (ink on paper). It's a sure-fire way to have our subconscious minds go after what we want to manifest in our lives even while we sleep. I encourage you to start a personal journal and write a little each day. This should be a personal diary for your eyes only. Be specific about your feelings and about what you want in life. There is no perfect way to journal. Everyone has their own style and format. I recommend writing about your desires, dreams, wishes and "feelings". Being able to address how you feel about emotional issues is the start to emotional maturity. You can, and should, journal about anything and everything. Nothing should be off limits. The benefit of keeping a succinct journal is realized when you go back and read what you wrote a year ago, realizing how you have grown and changed over time. Every day when I finish journaling, I'm always excited to return to the entry from a year ago to see how I've changed and grown. This will absolutely help with your ongoing quest to reach emotional and spiritual maturity as discussed in Section III of this book. Journaling is key to acquiring self-actualization, the final goal of a strategic plan for your life. This needs to become one of your high-value activities.

PICTURE BOARDING

Your subconscious mind cannot determine between what's real and what's not. It deals with whatever is presented. Is a picture real or not? Your conscious mind can tell the difference between a picture of a beautiful car and a real car. Your subconscious mind can't. So, what happens if you present a lot of pictures to your sub conscious mind? Your subconscious mind, wants to manifest whatever it sees. When teaching goal setting techniques, I have my students construct picture boards of desired goals. This exercise helps focus the subconscious mind on obtaining whatever it sees. The more vivid the picture, the more likely your subconscious mind will lead you to obtaining what it sees. A great exercise in my opinion. Many mentees have large picture boards of goals they hope to obtain. Your mind will manifest whatever you focus on and what you think about the most. I encourage you to build a picture board filled with heart desires and look/gaze at it often. Many students have boards hanging in their offices and/or homes with pictures of material things like summer homes, cars, clothes, swimming pools, vacation destinations, etc. in addition to esoteric goals of things like a beautiful family, spiritual references, great job, etc. Picture boarding energizes your subconscious mind and needs to become one of your high-value activities.

If one of your goals is to make a lot of money, remember this quote: "Education and growth are much more important than money". If embraced, you will have all the money you need, but you first must embrace education and growth. I believe this is true.

Another quote to consider: "All hard work brings profit, but mere talk leads only to poverty." Proverbs 14:23.

NOTEBOOK

Create a sacred notebook with all the items recommended in this book. Your goals, your goal statements, your triggers, your mantras, your unique ability, your mission statement, your passion statement, your picture board, etc. This is all the information I'm going to list as I want you to take personal responsibility for creating a phenomenal notebook for your own life. Take 100% responsibility for building a great product that will lead and direct your life from this day forward. Reading it daily and keeping it close by like sacred ancient scripture. Your personal road map to success.

CONCLUSION

These preceding items are the ones that have helped me most in my career. There are an unlimited number of topics that could be incorporated into a strategic plan depending on your role in life. Most of the suggestions listed here are for people in corporate America. Obviously, a stay at home mom, minister, teacher, dentist, day laborer, etc., would all have a different set of topics included in their personal strategic plan, but the process is the same and works regardless of your profession. (i.e. Understanding and implementing The Mind-Body Crossover, Future Pacing, The Countdown, creative visualization, imprinting, triggers, unique ability and the power of repetition is the key to success).

It takes time to form new habits and to incorporate a new way of living. The key here is not to become discouraged if you "fall off the wagon" from time-to-time. Remember, repetition is the key to success when forming new habits. Be kind and understanding to yourself and keep rebooting whenever necessary. This is a long journey but well worth the ride! This is the end of Section II. You now have the knowledge to build a plan to help acquire the success, money and power to realize Maslow's first rung his hierarchy of food, shelter, clothing, etc.

Section III will teach you how to acquire the maturity level necessary to truly enjoy the success, money and power you gained in this section. Stay focused.

NOTE: Have you noticed that I have labeled several items in this book as: "high-value activities"? Whenever you give, an important name or title to a topic, it helps add significance to the activity by telling your subconscious mind this is an important task that needs to be remembered and repeated. It reinforces the importance of the activity for internalization of whatever you name as important. Your subconscious mind will handle the rest. Use this technique in journaling and writing.

CHAPTER SUMMARY

 GOLDEN NUGGETS:

- The formal, strategic planning process was just starting to catch on for smaller mid-sized companies in the early seventies.

- The differences between a strategic plan for business and for personal are subtle yet transformative.

- A personal mission statement provides clarity and gives you a sense of purpose.

- Once your conscious mind is fed the basics of your desires, your subconscious mind will work to achieve them, even while you sleep!

- If you are serious about personal growth, you must have "quiet" time to grow and mature.

- It is imperative that you let your calendar control your life. It will force you to act, which is key for implementing a strategic plan for your life.

- I'm convinced that rising to the level of one's incompetency is considered a must to land a "C Suite" position at many companies.

- Never assume your boss knows what he is doing! Always act as though he does!!

- Never "bad mouth" anyone and never, never, ever gossip (with anyone, anywhere)!

- Once you get a job, be honest, ethical and moral, and you will eventually reach the top.

- Remember that great companies always pay for performance, leadership and value. Bring all three if you really want to succeed.

- Most marriage counselors will tell you that the "in love" stage lasts eighteen months, and you can't think clearly during this stage! To fully and completely understand your significant other, to truthfully understand if you are a good fit for each other, you must be out of the "in love" stage.

- Everyone loves a great speaker.

- Being able to speak in front of others is a tool that will give you a huge advantage in the marketplace.

- Public speaking - Every good strategic plan should include becoming proficient at this skill. Feel the fear and do it anyway!

- I recommend all my mentees join a service organization, and I get them on the "Free Lunch" Program to ascertain the best fit for their individual personalities.

- If you truly want to be a leader and a winner, get involved with a good service organization and give back to your community! No life is complete without service. Be kind and give, give, give!

- Highly successful entrepreneurs are usually heavily involved with shaping their respective industries.

- You can be distracted, or you can be legendary, but you can't be both. The secret to genius is focus.

- Become an eternal learner!

- Personal mastery demands ample quiet time. No distractions. Just focus.

- Start every work day disconnected from social media and your phone and emails and focus on the one thing that will bring you closer to your major impact goal.

- It takes time to form new habits and to incorporate a new way of living. The key here is, not to become discouraged if you "fall off the wagon" from time-to-time.

- Buck cards accelerate and reinforce goal achievement through repetition.

- Journaling is the simplest way to bridge The Mind-Body Crossover.

- Picture boarding bridges the gap using visual images.

- Buck cards, journaling and picture boarding need to become high-value activities to help ensure your success.

- Hesitation kills!

ACTION ITEMS: (TELL ME WHAT TO DO)

- Write your personal mission statement as outlined

- Write seven major goals, one for each area of your life.

- Set a calendar reminder to review and rewrite these goals every month.

- Implement Rise and Shine, starting tomorrow.

- Fill your calendar with all standing events as outlined.

- Implement the Free Lunch Program by attending your first free lunch this week. Join a service organization in the next 60 days.

- Join a Toastmasters Club this week.

- Join your career industry association before the end of the month.

- Buy your first book on tape and listen to it in your car today. Set a tickler on your calendar to buy or download audio recordings to listen to on your iPad, iPhone, etc. and start a program of learning one hour every day.

- When exercising, never go for a long run or work-out without listening to something motivation or educational. I call this Running College! Learn from people who have already done it! Collapse the learning timeline.

- Buy buck cards and use as outlined.

- Buy a journal and start journaling every day for the rest of your life.

- Build a picture board as outlined and place in your office.

- Create a sacred notebook with all the items recommended in this book.

SECTION III

REACHING FOR
SELF-ACTUALIZATION

CHAPTER ELEVEN

HAPPINESS VS. JOY

When we complete building a strategic plan for our life as outlined in the previous chapters and implement the strategies and techniques discussed, we will have a road map on how to solve the success, money, power challenge. Now in Section III we are focused on acquiring the emotional skills necessary to attain what Maslow labels as Self-Actualization. These skills will provide the maturity and mental skills necessary to help us fully enjoy the success, money and power acquired in Section II. This section is focused on our mental state, capacities and capabilities. The goal is spiritual and mental in nature. It starts with a mental adjustment in how we think, act and react. It's about our attitude and what we really want out of life. Happiness or joy?

I mentioned earlier the definition of the two words happiness and joy. They hold two very different meanings in my opinion. I hope this story gives you a different perspective of viewing life and how to react to the emotional ups and downs we all face in our journey. Here we start a journey to self-actualization.

What are you looking for in life? What's it all about? Most of us would probably say we are looking for "happiness" in our lives when expressed in a non-judgmental way. We think we are searching for happiness, but I believe we are searching for something much deeper and much more fulfilling. I want to explore these two words, so you can obtain a deeper, richer sense of the word "joy". Happiness in my opinion, is a fun word expressing the lighter, fun side of life that brings instant gratification without much commitment or emotional awareness. In other words, I could say Sex, Drugs, Rock-N-Roll can bring you instantaneous happiness. Joy, on the other hand, is a more emotional word expressing both positive and negative emotions. You don't experience sadness when you are talking about happiness, but you might have a tremendous amount of joy when you are experiencing sadness. Joy is a deeper, more meaningful experience than happiness. Happiness is a matter of experiencing your desires and something needs to happen to produce it. Joy is something that springs from the spirit within which needs no external stimuli. It is the state of well-being that surfaces even during apparent sadness or adversity.

Example: Let's say you just graduated from high school and are off to college in another town. After three weeks at school you come home to visit and notice your mother is limping around the house. You ask her what's wrong and she says, "Oh my back is out of alignment. I need to go see the chiropractor but just don't have the time". You say, "Mom you need to go get adjusted". Four weeks later you come home for another visit, notice that she is limping worse than before and make another inquiry. She again says she hasn't had the time. You return to school and come back three weeks later, and she is having great difficulty walking, complaining about sciatic nerve pain and starting to drag her left leg. You immediately grab your dad and the two of you take her to see the chiropractor. She gets up on the examining table and the chiropractor starts to examine your mom. Surprisingly he looks at your mom and says, "Mrs. Dawson you are in good alignment. I can't find anything wrong! I think you should go see your medical doctor!" The three of you are shocked and head to the medical center immediately. After a three-hour, complicated set of tests, the doctors tell your family that your mom is very sick. They found five tumors in her back that were causing the pain and they tested positive for cancer. An additional body scan found three black spots on her kidneys and two more spots on her brain. All in advance stages of cancer.

Over the next several months your mother continues to deteriorate. She does not respond to treatment and after several surgeries, the doctors have little hope for her survival. After nine months, she is bedridden and on morphine to help with pain. She continues to be in a tremendous amount of pain for another six months and continues to slowly deteriorate. Totally incontinent and in tremendous pain, she is finally placed in hospice care after nineteen months, and finally dies. Are you happy? No, of course not, she is your mom! Are you sad? Yes, of course she is your mom! Do you have any joy? Yes, because she is no longer in pain and probably in a better place. You are also thankful that she is no longer suffering. In the traditional sense of the word we don't often think of this situation as a "joyful" event, but the circumstance of the situation gives us a different understanding and comprehension of the word joy. It's a more complicated, emotional word than happiness. I've given this lengthy example to help you consider what really brings you contentment. I have been guilty of chasing "happiness" instead of "joy". When you visit the book of Galatians 5:22-23 in the New Testament of the Bible, the fruits of the spirit are listed as: love, joy, peace, forbearance, kindness, goodness, faithfulness, gentleness and self-control. You will notice that "happiness" is not listed as one of the gifts of the Spirit, while joy is listed. Enough said!

Today, I find contentment by focusing on the value of both the good and the bad. Sadness can sometimes bring peace and joy if I look at the situation in a different light. Joy comes from within and success follows - not the other way around.

When faced with situations like the one above, it makes me realize how grateful I am for not having to deal with such difficulties. Being grateful is a personal goal I try to focus on every day. I'm convinced that, "Gratefulness is the great multiplier of all great things to come". I'm not sure where I heard this quote but whenever I stop focusing on myself and focus on helping others, my life improves exponentially. The more grateful I am, the greater things are that come my way. I love this mantra! I encourage you to embrace it as well. "Gratefulness is the great multiplier of all great things to come". Start being grateful for everything you have and watch your life improve! Give up self-pity, victimization, passive aggressive behavior and resentments. Start experiencing, accepting and feeling your emotions. It's all about attitude!

It's all about joy!

CHAPTER SUMMARY

 GOLDEN NUGGETS:

- We think we are searching for happiness, but I believe we are searching for something deeper and more fulfilling.

- Happiness, in my opinion, is a fun word that expresses the lighter side of life that brings instant gratification without much commitment or emotional awareness. i.e. Sex, Drugs, & Rock & Roll.

- Joy, on the other hand, is a more emotional word that express both positive and negative emotions.

- Joy is something that springs from the spirit within and needs no external stimuli. It is the state of well-being that surfaces even during apparent sadness or adversity.

- In the Bible, you will notice that "happiness" is not listed as one of the gifts of the Spirit, while joy is listed.

- "Gratefulness is the great multiplier of all great things to come".

- Whenever I stop focusing on myself and focus on helping others, my life improves exponentially.

- Hesitation kills!

ACTION ITEMS: (TELL ME WHAT TO DO)

- Add a listing to your weekly calendar at the start of the week, Monday morning and make a list of what you are grateful for today. Doing this assignment will enhance your outlook on the week ahead and get you started with a positive attitude to face the world. Very powerful. I suggest you make this a high-value activity.

CHAPTER TWELVE

THE MARCH TO MATURITY

At some point in our lives we all must grow up and face realities. Here is a statement/question for your consideration: "Self-examination is an honest, hard look at the realities of your existing situation and an in-depth, serious look at how you got to where you are and what your part was in the process." I call this, The March to Maturity. We must acknowledge our shame and our guilt! Shame, relates to who we really are, and guilt relates to what we've really done! Some individuals seem to arrive at this point earlier than others, but it is a necessary process regardless of how, when and where the "teacher" appears. "The unexamined life is not worth living"-Plato. The goal is: pure joy!

I fumbled around a lot in life, never taking seriously the need to really grow up. I was more concerned with experiencing what I labeled as, "Happiness" (Sex, Drugs, Rock-N-Roll, Whiskey and More – More Money, More Power, More Prestige, etc.). I should have been more focused on "Joy" i.e. Peace, Serenity, Love, Hope, Understanding, etc. My addictive behavior and entrepreneurial spirit, along with a get rich quick mentality did not serve me very well early on in life. I was all about instant gratification. I fought growing up with a vengeance. However, once I realized and accepted responsibility for my character defects, I had an intense passion to grow and blossom, starting an unending quest for spiritual maturity on an ongoing and everlasting basis. Today my life is filled with pure joy and I am in a constant "Joy" quest to gain a higher level of spiritual maturity!

As mentioned earlier, I suffer from a clinically diagnosed attention deficit disorder and an addictive personality. Not much fun. This combination can wreak havoc, without proper medication and or proper psychological awareness and assistance. My addictive behavior led to chronic alcoholism at an early age and a malady I suffered with untreated until I was sixty years old. I had my first drink of alcohol at age twelve and knew immediately I liked the effects of this drug. It was a destructive, debilitating, controlling factor in my life every waking moment and a huge burden to carry. Today, through the help of a twelve-step program I now know it is a disease. A killing, indiscriminate disease, if not treated, it will put you in the grave!

"Knowing your own darkness is the best method for dealing with the darkness's of other people." — Carl Gustav Jung, 1875-1961, Swiss psychiatrist and psychoanalyst who founded analytical psychology.

May 31st, is the last day of National Mental Health Awareness Month, which was established in 1949 by the Mental Health America organization, then known as the National Association of Mental Health. It is estimated that at least 20 percent of Americans, including some in prominent and influential positions of significant trust and responsibility, suffer from some form of mental ill health and/or personality disorder. This basically says that one out of every five people we meet has some form of mental health issue. We need to be more aware of the condition of our fellow man and work harder to understand those afflicted.

Most psychologist have their patients focus on what happened to them before the age of seventeen to help understand their emotional state. Most of us act the way we act because of what happens to us in early childhood or adolescence. Being able to identify the traumatic events of our early life will explain a lot about who we are and why we act the way we act. This is called self-examination.

Today, I'm convinced that you cannot fully enjoy life without an in-depth exploration and self-examination. I personally learned a lot about myself through a twelve-step program. If you really want to experience life to the fullest you must continue to grow, addict or not. It starts with a process of awareness and ends with humility and integrity. Many times, life throws us into difficult situations that force us to stop, listen, learn or die. It's a maturation process. I see the process as a five-part progression as outlined below. If you are suffering from addiction of any kind, there is a tremendous amount of hope if you are willing to face reality and get help! Regardless of your existing condition, physically healthy or addictively sick, a better life is assured by working on this five-step process to obtain a higher level of maturity and humility. I'm talking about improving our emotional intelligence, (EQ). Setting our new moral compass. Living a life of integrity. Your body, mind, spirit and soul know when you are out of alignment with integrity. You can't hope to heal until you address these issues requiring 100% honesty, self-discovery and growth. It takes hard work! Here are the five steps to discovering a life of joy.

A PROCESS OF MATURING:

Step 1: Self-awareness

Step 2: Emotional awareness

Step 3: Emotional maturity

Step 4: Spiritual awareness

Step 5: Spiritual maturity

I am continually amazed that our educational system totally ignores instruction in human emotion, human behavior and moral psychology. In my opinion, it's the single most catastrophic shortfall in our global education system. I'm convinced that society in general could be greatly improved and benefited if we mandated human behavior curriculum at every level of education and taught individuals how to be aware of and in control of their emotions. In my opinion, the five steps outlined in this chapter regarding, progression to maturity, need to be taught starting at a young age. Individuals need to be made aware of their emotions and how to handle and express feelings in a constructive and productive way to avoid unchecked anger and manipulation. Uncontrolled anger and hate are destroying our world due to the manipulation of the masses. Being cognizant of one's maturity level, or lack thereof, is critical to one's emotional health and success in life. Unfortunately, I'm fully aware that the "Wealthy Elite" would never allow this to happen as it would prevent the ongoing "dumbing-down" of the populace and would prevent the wholesale control of the masses. It is the number one way for the wealthy elite to maintain power and control over the masses and the need to perpetuate the welfare state.

Regardless of your political stance, or belief system regarding this issue, I encourage you to look at your personal level of maturity. Work to train yourself and your offspring about self-awareness, emotional awareness, emotional maturity, spiritual awareness and spiritual maturity. I'm convinced that once an individual fully understands human emotion and behavior and takes 100% responsibility for their own actions, they naturally grow towards becoming "givers" instead of "takers". This act, works to eliminate the welfare state, as people naturally start to take care of each other and no longer rely on the government to provide for their needs. Prior to FDR and The Social Security Act, there was no safety net for individuals and we took care of one another. In my opinion, we were a much kinder and gentler nation. Today the Wealthy Elite promise unlimited welfare to get votes and control the populace by appealing to their warped since of maturity (i.e. immaturity), lack of self-awareness, lack of emotional maturity and their lack of education. Politicians are master manipulators at preying on the emotionally immature and uneducated to promote their social and political agendas. The emotional rhetoric of Adolph Hitler being a good example of this type of manipulation in the 20th Century. Don't be a victim of this manipulative control mechanism used by the wealthy elite. It starts by understanding your unique ability. This is accomplished by understanding who you are and your personality and how it works. This requires assessment testing. As mentioned earlier I highly recommend the Birkman Method for you and your children as an excellent assessment tool.

STEP ONE: SELF-AWARENESS

Self-awareness is the first step in the maturation process. So many of us are not aware of very much and have not given much consideration to what makes us tick. We are not even aware of ourselves. We are existing in a state of "duh"! We are just going with the flow, letting life take us where it will. Thinking we have no control over our lives or our futures, we are only a "victim". We are just letting life happen to us. Often, we are satisfied with Sex, Drugs & Rock-N-Roll, with little or no ambition! For most of us this lethargic existence is most prevalent in our teens and early twenties. For some, unfortunately, it lasts a lifetime. Content to let life pass us by and never taking 100% responsibility for what happens to us in life, because we think we have no control. What is 100% responsibility, you may ask? Sometimes we are lazy, spoiled or just don't give a damn! We look for someone else to take care of us and refuse to accept reality. We refuse to take responsibility for what happens to us in every area of our lives. Always looking for someone else to blame, we wallow in self-pity, victimization, and passive aggressive behavior always filled with excuses and blaming others. Never facing up to our own responsibilities. Always plotting revenge against those who hurt us. Many times, addiction is the root cause of this debilitating attitude but often it is just fear, laziness or an entitlement attitude. Regardless, we must face the fear and become 100% responsible for ourselves. No one else is going to take responsibility for us. Because of this condition, we usually never ask ourselves the "tough" questions.

"Why" vs. "How" Questions

The universe seldom answers questions starting with "why". A "why" question only makes one aware of an existing situation or a reality. It seldom can create an enlightening or positive answer. It is informative but disempowering. Its only value is to reveal a situation that we have ultimately created ourselves (or that someone else put us in) but seldom creates an answer to the situation. Conversely, a "how" question creates an avenue for exploration and can be very empowering. It challenges us to face the reality of a situation and act to produce a positive result. "How" questions promote and create healing.

Both types are what I call "tough" questions and have a purpose.

We never really stop and consider the tough questions:

- <u>Why</u> was I abused as a child?
- <u>How</u> can I overcome my abuse as a child?
- <u>Why</u> am I so sad?
- <u>How</u> can I be happy more of the time?
- <u>Why</u> am I so mad and angry?
- <u>How</u> can I prevent being mad and angry?

Other questions for consideration:

- What is my purpose for living?
- What is my responsibility in life?
- How do I fit into the overall scheme of life?
- Why do I act the way I act?
- Why am I in this condition?
- Why do I think the way I think?
- Why am I so lucky?
- Why am I so unlucky?
- What do I care about?
- What do I want out of life?
- Where am I going?
- Why do I feel so insecure?
- What am I passionate about?
- Who do I care about?
- Who cares about me?
- Why do I feel so hopeless?

Never asking any of these questions is what I label the "walking-dead" or "brain-dead" syndrome. Starting to explore these questions is the baseline starting point to becoming a mature, functioning, humble individual. When we start taking a 100% responsibility for ourselves we begin to realize we have never seriously considered any of the above questions, much less the answers. Often, we get stuck in this state due to fear and can't find a way out until a catastrophic event crushes us and forces us into reality, or we just have an epiphany because of some related or unrelated incident. Being crushed hurts and most of us would rather live without any seasons of pain. Yet during such times, God often does His greatest work in our lives, reshaping and realigning us for His divine purposes. "Consciousness of self is what ultimately leads to oneness/ wholeness with God and the universe." -Emmet Fox. It requires self-forgiveness, self-awareness and humility. To master the universe, we must start by being aware of our resentments and self-pity, as they lead us to anger and anger leads to fear. Fear is not God based. Love is God based.

Many times, we find ourselves in this state because we lack self-discipline or self-denial. I call these, Discipline and Denial, the Two D's.

At some point, we hopefully wake up and realize we want more out of life. We start the maturation on our own or as the result of an "event" or a thought. Usually, our first realization is that we must take responsibility for our own state, because no one else is going to do it for us. This comes when we realize we can't have any real joy without discipline or denial. We start to see the benefit of these two states. Hard work produces profit and requires that we become disciplined and that we deny instant gratification if we truly want long term satisfaction, peace and joy. I encourage you to embrace the Two D's!

"Self-awareness is a great tool to combating resistance. When you feel resistance to taking action, stop in your tracks. Try to understand the 'why' behind it. Is the resistance valid?"
— <u>Vatsala Shukla</u>, <u>Get Noticed! 15 Insider Tips guaranteed to improve your Executive Presence</u>

STEP TWO: EMOTIONAL AWARENESS

Emotional awareness is the second step in the maturation process. Here we start to understand and become aware of our emotional states and how we react to emotion, moment by moment. We begin to realize we are victims of our emotions. We begin to realize that emotions drive our behavior. However, we first must be aware they even exist. In this stage, we become aware they do exist, and we are usually their victim due to a lack of knowledge about how they affect us, and we also start acknowledging that we are generally living in a state of fear.

Here are eleven examples of emotional states/awareness that can cause us to live miserable lives, until we recognize their existence and begin to humble ourselves:

1. Resentments
2. Self-pity
3. Victimization
4. Passive Aggressive Behavior
5. Always being critical of others
6. Plotting revenge
7. Argumentative Nature
8. Rather get even than get ahead
9. Blaming others
10. Rather be right than happy

11. Gossip

Most of our emotional deficiencies are centered in resentments. When we get "naked" with the truth we all have resentments we carry around that can cause us to behave in an immature fashion. If you are serious about growing to emotional maturity, you must first recognize your resentments. You need maturity to grow past your resentments and it starts with self-awareness.

You must name your resentments, take responsibility for them, and work to adjust and correct your behavior. My first step on this journey required me to realize that I cannot be right 100% of the time. I've come to realize that life is balanced in all areas. Hot-cold, right-wrong, happy-sad, white-black, top-bottom, etc. It is a law of nature that we can only be right 50% of the time. Sometimes we might be right 100% in a certain situation, but we will also be 100% wrong in another. It always balances out to exactly 50-50. Once we get outside of our ego and admit we have faults and defects, we can start to grow. We start by identifying and naming the resentments and defects. This is a challenging task for most as it's the first time for many of us to admit some character faults to ourselves. It's an assault on our own ego! Have we "BUMPED OUR HEADS"! This takes a lot of guts! We might have to fake it till we make it. Or, how about, "Acting our self into a new way of thinking!"

I had to finally realize I must surrender, fully surrender if I want to join the winning team! Life will take on a new meaning when we start to mature, when we start to grow up. The arrogance to think you are always right, yields a sad, immature existence! Stop assuming you are right. Instead assume you might/could be wrong. It's a good start to emotional maturity and humility. The point is not what you do or what you accomplish, but who you are. A taker or a giver? A consumer or a provider. An idiot or a guru?

190

This knowledge could jump start your Life into the next step:

STEP THREE: EMOTIONAL MATURITY

Emotional maturity is the third step in the maturation process. Reaching emotional maturity requires us to not only be aware of our emotions and short comings, but to do something with the knowledge. The biggest roadblock to emotional maturity is what I call, "Bondage of Self!" It is taking responsibly for and recognizing that we are slaves to our own egos. It's recognition that we think about ourselves way too often! It's recognition that we think way too little about our fellow man. It is recognizing that we are all fear-based creatures with little or no understanding of humility!

We must learn to take 100% responsibility for what happens to us. I like to call this step, "developing an intentional relationship with your mind." We must take active responsibility for our thoughts. What is a thought? I believe it is a speculation, an unchecked reason, an unexplored possibility. It's nothing until we stop and analyze it. We must learn to recognize when a new thought enters our consciousness and analyze it immediately and appropriately. Don't believe everything you think! We must program our minds to constantly be aware of where we are on the emotional curve, whenever a new thought pops into our minds. Don't let a thought attach to an emotion before you analyze it.

Acquiring emotional maturity is no easy task. Intellectually we are trained to think and react. This is an ineffective and incomplete way to exist, as it ignores feelings and emotions. To be a complete individual we must deal with our emotions and our feelings in addition to thinking and acting. We need to be aware of our feelings but also be cognizant that feelings are not necessarily facts! We must become experts at what I call, "observing-without-reacting." We must become experts at analyzing cause and effect with a focus on our feelings and emotions. We must practice becoming stoic, when observing emotional/volatile situations. Vocabulary.com Dictionary defines: "Being stoic is being calm and almost without emotion. When you're stoic, you don't show what you're feeling, and you also accept whatever is happening. The noun stoic connotates a person who's not very emotional. The adjective stoic describes any person, action or thing that seems emotionless and almost blank. Mr. Spock, from the oldest Star Trek show, was a great example of a stoic person: He tried to never show his feelings. Someone yelling, crying, laughing or glaring is not stoic. Stoic people calmly go with the flow and don't appear to be shook up by much. You know you are becoming emotionally mature when you can master this technique. It takes extreme discipline to fully master. I like to say that: "I have evolved from fast and furious to slow and curious". A great quote from my buddy J.C. It's emblematic of what happens to a person when they make mega leaps in emotional growth and maturity.

We also need the ability to look at every situation and ask ourselves, "What part, if any, did I play in the situation?" This requires emotional awareness. This requires a lot of anger management and future pacing. Our resentments can cause us to act like idiots and get us in trouble whenever we act without thinking. Acknowledge and check your ego all day, every day, moment by moment!

I resent people who cut me off in traffic. My immediate response is honk, holler, scream and try to go around the culprit to try to cut him off! I would rather get even than get ahead! What an idiot. A better response is to wonder why the person cut me off in the first place. Does he have a dying child in the front seat and is desperately trying to get to a hospital? Is he drunk and irresponsible? Is he an arrogant asshole? Regardless of the answer, the emotionally mature reaction is to not react, only observe and go on with your life and learn from the occurrence. This reaction requires a lot of self-control, practice and emotional maturity.

Another extreme example is what happens when I find out my wife is having an affair with my next-door neighbor. My first extreme response might be to grab a gun and... A better response is to ask "Why", "What caused this to happen?" A better question might be to ask, "What was my part in this situation? Have I been a horrible spouse? Have I been taking her for granted? What was my part?" Then ask yourself some empowering "how" questions. i.e. How can I be a better husband? How can we repair the damage? How do we move on from here?

When faced with emotional flare ups we must immediately stop, analyze and future pace. Resentments cause fear and anger to surface quickly as we are fear-based creatures. It's in our DNA. Usually we are naturally in fear of losing what we have or not getting what we want. This is the normal reaction of most people when a resentment raises its ugly head. When grabbing a gun in the example above, it might help to future pace and possibly see yourself in prison for the rest of your life or other horrible futures created by acting without thinking. I repeat, we must become experts at observing-without-reacting.

When I'm up, I'm up and when I'm down, I'm down. Why? We must train ourselves to ask more "Why Questions" even though they are disempowering. As mentioned earlier, "Why" questions do serve a purpose to help us experience reality and take responsibility for what happens to us in life. They make us look at ourselves with a critical eye that can be beneficial for emotional and spiritual growth. "Why" questions convict us and help humble our egos. A necessary step.

- Why did I get mad when that car cut me off?
- Why do I feel so insecure when….?
- Why did I overreact when he pushed my buttons?
- Why did I lie?
- Why do I feel the way I feel?
- Why am I drinking every day?
- Why am I arrogant?
- Why do I embellish?
- Why do I gossip?
- Why am I so critical of my children?
- Why do my moods change?
- Why do I feel so unlucky?
- Why do I hate?
- Why do I blame others?
- Why am I smoking marijuana?
- Why do I cheat on my husband?
- Why do I always feel sorry for myself?
- Why don't I take 100% responsibility for my life?
- Why am I looking at pornography?
- Why am I sad?
- Why don't I admit my mistakes?
- Why do I lust after other women?
- Why am I taking pain pills?
- Why am I angry?
- Why do I make excuses?
- Why am I drinking and driving?

There are a thousand more beneficial "Why Questions" tied to our emotional states. We must learn to embrace our emotional states and understand what causes us to feel the way we feel. Cause and effect! We need to start accepting the feelings and dealing with them appropriately instead of being controlled by our out of control emotions and ego. This requires a lot of introspection and above all a lot of honesty and humility! It requires us to stop and think before we act or react. Being able to admit mistakes and work on self-control moment by moment. It requires us to stop, listen, shut up and repeat! (The unexamined life is not worth living – Plato).

> "Answers come from questions, and the quality of any answer is directly determined by the quality of the question. Ask the wrong question, get the wrong answer. Ask the right question, get the right answer. Ask the most powerful question possible, and the answer may be life altering."— From the 2013 book, The One Thing, by Gary Keller, American entrepreneur, author and founder of Keller Williams Realty International.

Most emotional conflict is a result of frustration created by expectations not being met. This is a communication shortfall. Setting clear and reasonable expectations is critical to strong emotional health and great relationships. It starts with asking good questions as mentioned above. If you are struggling in your marital relationship or your work relationships, it probably is a result of not setting clear expectations. If you have plans to marry, I strongly suggest that you and your future spouse each create a list of 25 things you "expect" from your spouse in your marriage. Share these with your spouse and your marriage counselor prior to your trip down the aisle. If you are a boss, I suggest that you publish what you expect from your employees and discuss in detail with all your direct reports. It would also be advisable for your employees to disclose what they expect from you as their boss. Asking these questions upfront will save you a lot of grief in the long run and help immeasurably in your emotional growth and maturity.

Arrogance versus humility is the battleground of the ego. Our egos can be a very destructive force in our lives if they go unnoticed and unchecked. We must stop thinking that we are right 100% of the time. Young executives climbing the corporate ladder often struggle with this dilemma. They mistakenly think that being decisive, demanding and commanding is the sign of great leadership. They are making decisions for decisions sake, to appear in command. Big mistake. When I was 30 years old, I had a 32-year-old boss who struggled with an out of control ego. He thought he was right all the time. He did not understand the Law of Averages. His insecurities were "showing" big time! He never considered that he might be wrong. He thought people were weak if they pondered possibilities. I suggest, you always start out with the premise that your thought pattern might be flawed and look for feedback and confirmation before charging down the road. Be a true Guru, not a true Idiot! Never make the arrogant mistake of thinking that you are always right!

We must be aware of these character defects if we truly want to grow. We must realize that we are fear-based beings, that it's in our DNA, and admit our insecurities if we truly want to excel at life. Sometimes in our stubbornness a catastrophic event is necessary, to humble us into facing realities of life head on with an honest assessment. I reached this point when I was sixty-two years old and finally faced the realities of my alcohol addiction and lack of emotional maturity. Emotion is a three-pronged enigma with a beginning, a middle and an end. I never used to accept or experience all three steps. I drank instead.

I was totally humbled by my addiction and had to admit that I was helpless against the disease of alcoholism. That was no easy pill to swallow, but recovery is a real possibility once you surrender and seek help. Humility is the starting point for recovery from our egos, regardless if we are an addict or not. It's all about emotional maturity and discovering the world does not revolve around me. "Humility is not thinking less of yourself, humility is thinking about yourself less!"

Obviously, this is easier said than done. It all starts with a self-examination of identifying our resentments. What's a resentment?

> Definition:
> the feeling of displeasure or indignation at some
> act, remark, person,etc., regarded as causing
> injury or insult.

Resentments come in many forms, and they have a considerable amount to do with our ego. I encourage you to make a list. When I first did this assignment, I came up with ten or eleven. Once my business coach fully explained the meaning of resentments, I could list about one hundred and sixty-five! Below is a short list of some random resentments, to give you an idea of what they might look like to you. I resent:

- People that gossip
- Arrogance in others
- People that cut me off in traffic
- Racists
- Loud talkers
- Body piercing

- People who are lazy
- Soft talkers
- People who are over achievers
- People who are under achievers
- People who use foul language
- Individuals that embellish
- Goody two shoes
- Jesus freaks
- Chauvinists
- Neat freaks
- Guys who cheat on their wives
- Undisciplined children
- Gals that cheat on their husbands
- Conservatives
- Atheists
- A clean house
- Agnostics
- Liberals
- Long hair
- Short hair
- Takers
- Kind people
- Givers
- People that think they know everything
- Bald people
- People who think they are always right
- Beards
- Angry people
- Cheaters

- People who speed on the highway
- Mohawk haircuts
- Whites
- Purple hair
- Asians
- Haters
- Blacks
- Tall people
- Midgets
- Hispanics
- Lovers
- Republicans
- Short people
- Democrats
- Dread locks
- Christians
- A dirty house
- Graffiti
- Skinny people
- A smelly car
- Smokers
- Fat people
- Loud movie theaters
- Pink
- Street people
- Buddhists
- Panhandlers
- Muslims
- Tattoos

- Celebrities
- Politicians
- Environmentalists
- Police
- Professional athletes
- Elitists

The list goes on and on. Once you identify the things you resent, you can start to evaluate the validity of each and take responsibility for your thoughts and actions regarding each resentment. Humans are for the most part "fear-based". You will quickly come to realize that most of your resentments are a result of your ego, prejudices, insecurities and fears. Being able to conquer one's resentments boils down to transforming from "taker" to "giver". Stop being a consumer and a complainer! It is a necessary step if you want to heal and grow! You will be able to recognize your growth when you realize you can finally "observe" without "reacting". It means taking responsibility for your thoughts and analyzing them before you react. Think before you speak. This confirms you are on the road to emotional maturity.

The most immature way to exist is to be a taker. (Lowest Maturity = What can you do for me? What's in it for me?) The second most immature existence is what I call give-to-get. i.e. I'll give you something only if you give me something in return. The next highest level of maturity is give-to-give. i.e. I like the feeling I get when I help someone else (giving), so I continue to help (to give). In other words, I give, to give, to give. These levels of maturity are also identified as Win-Lose, Lose-Win and Win-Win. Most everyone seems to think Win-Win is the highest level of maturity, but I beg to differ. Under a Win-Win scenario, "I" must make sure that "you" don't win more than "me"! Win-Win can become very divisive because I must make sure you don't win more than me or get ahead of me! Win-Win requires you/us to keep score – Bad! It can promote distrust if you are not careful because the focus is on me, me, me, me, me. (A bad place to focus).

So, what is the highest level of maturity? It's what I call, "Looking for A Receiver." Under this scenario I'm in an "action" mode. All the other modes are "passive". Looking for a receiver requires me to hunt down people or situations that need assistance/help. It requires action on my part. Every time someone decides to give, someone must be found to receive. In other words, I like to say, you must give it away to keep it. i.e. keep serenity, keep peace, keep joy, etc. It requires action on my part, discipline and denial of self. i.e. The highest form of maturity, "Looking for a Receiver."

It can also be defined as Give to Keep! Only in human interaction does "giving away" increase what you have. You must give it away to keep it. In the material world, i.e. a business, when you spend your money it gets depleted. In the human relationship world, when we give it away, spend it, it multiplies back to us/you. Only when we empty ourselves, can we be filled again. Another favorite quote of mine: "The act of giving is the soul of living."-Loreen Arbus, American humanitarian and philanthropist.

Here is the **FIRST NUGGET**: You can't give, without receiving. i.e. The secret to getting is giving! Wow!

SECOND NUGGET: Be a generous receiver when someone gives something to you. If you don't allow yourself to receive, you're refusing the gifts of others! —and you shut down the flow! Don't do that!

One of the biggest reasons we fail to mature and heal is our subconscious minds want to hold on to our wounds. To heal and grow to emotional maturity we must give up our wounds. This is terrifying to many people as often we are addicted to our wounds and use them as coping mechanisms to avoid pain or difficult situations. This is driven by fear. Coming to terms with our wound(s) and letting go, takes practice, determination, guts and sometimes intense therapy. Our first step to recovery is recognizing we are holding on to a wound.

A good example of this syndrome might be a woman who lost a young child in a car accident 20 years ago. Obviously, this is a serious wound as losing a child is one of the most devastating things that can happen to a person. When confronted with a difficult or serious encounter with another human being, the woman will invariably find a way to bring her lost child into a difficult situation or conversation. This is a subconscious manipulation to gain sympathy, empathy or avoid conflict or confrontation. It prevents emotional maturity.

"Wound-ology" is a term connoting this malady and a stumbling block to becoming emotionally mature. Keeping our wounds alive drains, us of precious energy. Our life force is being depleted when we relive our traumatic event. (a difficult divorce, loss of a loved one, bankruptcy, loss of a limb, loss of sight, abuse as a child, rape, addiction, etc.). Interestingly, we feel safe by revisiting these traumas and communicating with our wound even though it is secretly draining us of our life force. Wounds can change the way we see the world. Many people become jaded by wounds if left untreated often becoming overly pessimistic with a doomsday attitude about everything in life. They constantly speak negativity into everything and every situation. This negative self-talk dooms undertaken endeavors. If you catch yourself looking at every situation from the dark side, you need to eradicate the wound by eradicating negative self-talk. Always remember negative attracts negative. Positive thinking attracts positive results. Never allow negative thoughts to dominate. Your subconscious mind believes what you tell it. Be careful with speech and even more careful with thought!

Holding on to a wound causes you to begin to lose your spirit. Your focus is one dimensional, i.e. your wound, at the cost of all else. Eventually your physical body will begin to show the effects. Asking disempowering questions like: "Why did this happen to me?", are detrimental. The universe will not answer this type question. Give it up. Instead, chart a new course for the future. Imagine yourself in a different future free of your wound(s). When healing we start to ask better questions and take 100% responsibility for recovery. Am I an optimist or a pessimist? Change your focus and demand positivity!

I suggest you take a few moments to identify any wounds you might have and any you have used more than four or five times. If you have a chronic wound that you have used hundreds or more times over an extended period, I suggest you seek professional help.

A discussion of emotional maturity is never completed without a full understanding of self-pity and victimization. These two culprits are major stumbling blocks in our growth towards Spiritual Maturity, the end goal. Until we humble ourselves and come face to face with our fears we can't grow. The first step is to realize that everyone on this earth is wounded. There are obviously different degrees of being wounded and different ways to look at the reality of its existence. I believe we all have this malady. Unfortunately, we tend to think we are "wounded" more than others! (Not necessarily, true) Please read the list below:

- I was physically abused as a child.
- My wife cheated on me.
- The government unlawfully confiscated my wealth.
- I had to work my way through college.
- Kids made fun of me at school.
- I was raped by my uncle.
- I was discriminated against because of my color.
- My teachers always played favorites at my expense.
- I grew up without enough food to eat.
- I was discriminated against because of my religion.
- I was beaten by my mother/father.
- My husband lost all our retirement.
- I was forced into prostitution at age ten.
- I was discriminated against because of my gender.
- I was ostracized at school.
- My wife gambled away my inheritance.
- I was emotionally tortured by my parents.
- I was starved.
- My boss lied about me to cover his mistakes.
- I was beaten.
- I came from a dirt-poor family.
- I was ugly.
- My parents were drug addicts.
- I was fat.
- I was born blind.
- I was persecuted for my faith.
- My partners stole me blind.
- My mom was a prostitute.
- I was wrongly convicted of murder.

- I was born lame.
- I was a victim of a drive by shooting.
- I was a "latch key" kid.
- I was born into the ghetto.
- I was manipulated by my boyfriend.
- I was lied to by the government.
- The IRS targeted me unjustly.
- I was possessed by the devil.
- I was persecuted for my beliefs.
- I was gang raped.

Some of these wounds are horrible, some less so. Being able to forgive the perpetrators and move on is no easy task! We can work on this for a lifetime and sometimes not be successful. However, forgiveness is how we free ourselves! Forgiving ourselves and forgiving others. No easy task! I mention these wounds to draw attention to the plight of others and our own. Do you fall into any of these or similar categories? I fully realize that not everyone has the same position in life and is treated equally. I do believe that we all have our demons to deal with and I was personally guilty of a lot of self-pity and victimization. I personally had eight of the misfortunes listed above and continued to blame others for my situation in life. What a waste of time! I finally realized that just about everyone was capable of "upping" me with their own set of horrible things. Not to mention that no one seemed to seriously care about my horrible situation! No one! It finally made me realize I had to take a 100% responsibility for what would happen to me in the future because no one else would.

The point of this list and discussion is to help each of us realize bad things happen to everybody. Regardless of our situation, we still must take 100% responsibility for what happens to us going forward because no one else will. Personally, it was not a pretty picture. I did not like what I saw in the mirror. It took me a long time to stop blaming others, to stop the pity parties and the victimization. Victims don't make it. Victims never make it. Victims don't recover. I finally realized if I continued to wallow in self-pity and victimization I only continued to suffer! I had to stop. I had to be humbled. I had to refuse to be a victim!

I often think of the plight of Helen Keller who was blind, deaf and dumb. What a horrific set of circumstances to overcome. She overcame each of these deficiencies and led an extraordinary, productive life. Did she have more joy or more sadness in her life than me? Think on that question for a moment.

Then ask yourself a tough question, "Do I suffer from self-pity or victimization?"

STEP FOUR: SPIRITUAL AWARENESS

Spiritual awareness is the fourth step in the maturation process. Once we come to terms with our own character faults, i.e. arrogance, self-pity, victimization, resentments, passive aggressive behavior, always being right, getting even instead of getting ahead, etc., we can start a new quest for enlightenment, a quest for Spiritual Awareness. I am not talking about religion here. That's another subject all together. I'm talking about a spiritual force, a higher power, another way of looking at the world we live in. It makes no difference if you are Hindu, Buddhist, Jew, Christian, Sikh, Unitarian or Muslim, etc. I'm talking about a belief system that recognizes there is a lot we don't know about the universe and the world we live in. I'm talking about the possibility of another realm, another possible dimension other than what we experience with our known senses. I'm talking about an intuition suggesting we do not exist by chance or have just evolved over the last billion years from some natural occurrences/evolution over time.

I personally do not believe that my iPad evolved from mixing together some dirt, water and sunshine. I believe there is a higher spiritual force that created everything in the universe.

> "Everyone who is seriously involved in the pursuit of science becomes convinced that a spirit is manifest in the laws of the universe — a spirit vastly superior to that of man, and one in the face of which we with our modest powers must feel humble." — Albert Einstein, 1879-1955, German-born theoretical physicist, writing in a letter to New York sixth-grader Phyllis Wright, January 24, 1936.

I happen to be a believer in a higher power, a God, a creator. I am not a pantheist. I was raised as a Christian, a believer in Jesus Christ, and I embraced this religion after a thorough investigation over the last fifty years. Unlike other religions listed above, it's the only mainstream religion where the creator died, came back to life and the event was witnessed by over five hundred people. A phenomenal event to say the least! This religion is based on a triune God, three gods in one (Father, Son and Holy Spirit). This subject of spiritual awareness deals with my personal belief in Christianity and in the third godhead of the trinity, The Holy Spirit. Being spiritually aware of a force other than physical matter, nature and random choice. Most religions have a spiritual set of parameters that emulate their belief system and I challenge and encourage you to embrace yours, regardless of what religion you personally accept, if you truly want to experience peace and serenity. Why do you believe what you believe? We all must ask ourselves this question.

In Christianity, the three-person godhead mirrors the three realms/states of existence in our world. Represented by male (physical), female (emotional) and spiritual (godhead). In Christianity, the godhead inhabits all three realms or states of being as the godhead is, omnipotent (all powerful), omniscient (all knowing) and omnipresent (present everywhere).

Your belief system is your belief system. I'm not trying to convince you, in this book, that my belief system is absolute. I'm only pitching the case for a spiritual force possibility. There are numerous books, thousands that you can read about religion. I'm only informing you of my personal belief and a spiritual awareness that I have been experiencing, in my search for significance. I encourage you to embrace the same possibility and start your own investigation.

I will leave you with this quote for consideration:

> ". . . there is no meaningful separation between sacred and secular, physical and psychic, human and divine. They are two sides of one coin. There is within every being an inherent longing for and capacity to experience this union. Everything really does 'belong' because all things are finally connected to the same Creator and thus to one another."— Richard Rohr, American author, speaker, Roman Catholic priest, and founder of the Center for Action and Contemplation, Albuquerque, New Mexico.

STEP FIVE: SPIRITUAL MATURITY

Spiritual maturity is the fifth and final step in the maturation process. "When we change our way of thinking, we change". "When we change our hearts, everything changes". Spiritual maturity is where we fully realize it's better to be a "giver" than a "taker". We realize we must forgive to be forgiven. Live and let live. We must surrender to "Win". It's a conscious realization that we are now different and are continuing to grow and expand into eternity. We have a new way of seeing the world. A better way to look at and observe the world we live in and the people we interact with. This final step in the maturation process runs to infinity. You can never actually reach the goal, as it is ever expanding. It's never over. It's a final state of ever expanding knowledge and experience and it is powered by pure joy!

Upon starting the unending quest for spiritual maturity, it easier to "see". Everything becomes evident. You see differently than those working on step one, two, three or four. It is clear how to help others grow on the maturity scale once you have grown through the process yourself. At this point we finally realize "it" doesn't get better, "I" get better. It's an inside job. It's an interior conversation. We are at the top of Maslow's Pyramid of "self-actualization". It's no longer about me, me, me, me, me. It's no longer about being right or getting even or getting ahead. We finally realize the opposite of being right is being free! Everything seems to become uncomplicated as we realize there is wisdom in simplicity. We finally start to ponder wisdom and spirituality. What is wisdom? What is spirituality? How do I get wisdom? How do I get spirituality? I think the answer to these questions comes from what I call, "Standing in The Fire"! It's a lot like being stoic (observing but not reacting). Author Richard Rohr put it best when he said: "Spirituality is about subtraction, not addition. Less is more". Simplicity reigns in this state. We finally surrender our lives to freedom! In other words, once we "surrender" we join the Winning Team. We must give it away to keep it. We receive when we give it away. Then wisdom, spirituality and simplicity manifest in our lives as we learn from the discipline and denial of "standing in the fire". It reminds me of a scripture found in the Christian Bible 2 Corinthians 12, "For when I am weak, then am I strong."

Total surrender demands that we consider and embrace a moral authority, a moral code and become aware of our moral compass. We must acknowledge to ourselves what we believe in and what we stand for and how we are going to live our lives. What are our standards? What are our absolutes? What are our self-governing rules? Are we going to embrace good or evil? To be complete we must address these moral issues. Are we going to live a sin free or a sinful life? It's our choice. It is interesting that we get the term "sin" from archery. It literally means to miss the mark. Are you going to live a spirit-filled life or a carnal life? Who and what is going to be your God? Your Higher Power? As you approach spiritual maturity you must face these questions to obtain spiritual maturity. It's a choice, it's your choice. It reminds me of the old Native American story of a warrior visiting with the medicine man asking for spiritual advice to deal with an interior battle he was struggling to overcome. He explained to the doctor that a battle was being waged in his mind during his dreams where a Black Wolf (Evil) and a White Wolf (Good) were fighting for supremacy of his being/soul/spirit and mind. He was curious and perplexed about the dream and wanted to know who was going to win the battle. His answer: "The one you feed"! ------ It's your choice!

We finally stop blaming others and take 100% responsibility for what happens to us in life. We no longer regret the past but appreciate it for the lessons we've learned. In other words, we must give up all hope of creating a better past! We also give up the self-pity, the victimization, the resentments, the passive aggressive behavior, etc. We make a conscious decision to stop living in hell on earth! We finally realize we are victims of a war we have waged against ourselves! We set ourselves free! Free to enjoy God's creation and the spiritual relationship he offers us. "Religion is for people who are afraid of going to hell. Spirituality is for people who've been there." I'm talking about living life on a much higher and intellectual plane. A higher level of maturity and an intense, intimate relationship with my/your creator.

My spiritual journey has been taking a lot of twist and turns as I continue to grow in humility. Coming to terms with my addiction has helped me build a personal relationship with my spiritual creator. I always used to resent "holier than thou" Bible thumpers who asked me if I had a "Personal Relationship" with Jesus Christ. I also, resented Buddhists who could meditate for many hours and talk about a spiritual connection I never could properly experience. As I continue to learn and grow spiritually, these statements no longer offend me. I have finally decided to give my life over to a higher power! To shift from living 100% in the carnal state to living in and experiencing the spiritual state. As mentioned earlier, I believe we are spiritual beings not human beings. I believe I will continue to grow and expand infinitely into the future when I leave this body and enter the next chapter. I believe I will experience an infinite number of new experiences forever. An infinite number of new colors. An infinite number of new musical notes. An infinite number of new sounds, smells, etc. Into infinitum with my higher power, my GOD.

I grew up as a child attending the Lutheran Church and today I am often invited to be a guest speaker at many different churches that would be classified as either "organized" or "spirit filled". I believe all churches/religious organizations have the potential/purpose to act as a stepping stone to help each of us experience GOD and grow spiritually, regardless if we attend an "organized" or "spirit filled" church. Today my church membership resides with a "spirit filled" church that has helped expand my God relationship exponentially. My spirituality took a mega leap when I was introduced to The Living Word Faith Center in Houston, Texas, pastored by Bishop John L. Hickman Jr. Bishop Hickman helped me experience spirituality as opposed to religion. He has led me to experience a personal relationship with my creator as opposed to a relationship with my religion. Today I am trying to live a life focused on the spiritual world as opposed to the carnal world. I'm continuing to work the Mind-Body Crossover every day and I now meditate, fast and pray because of my new spiritual life-skills and the process I've mastered to change my life. My arrogance and ego have been forced to make a big adjustment to help me live a life filled with joy, instead of a life filled with empty Sex, Drugs & Rock-N-Roll and MORE. I now live in peace, serenity and humility due to my new spirituality and The Mind-Body Crossover.

Today I try to live out my faith on a moment by moment basis, always trying to live as a spirit being instead of a carnal, human being. I profess my faith to others in a soft gentle way, always looking for a way to help others experience their personal God or their higher power. I witness daily about my personal belief system. Looking for a "receiver" every day and sharing with others how to witness numerous times every day to our fellow beings in a hurting world.

My spiritual maturity is growing and expanding daily. I am blessed indeed! I have become friends with my past as I ultimately know that I created it. The good and the bad, it's all mine! Guilt and shame! As mentioned earlier, (It makes no difference if you are a Hindu, Buddhist, Jew, Christian, Sikh, Unitarian or Muslim, etc.), I encourage you to experience "the spirit", not just religion.

CHAPTER SUMMARY

 GOLDEN NUGGETS:

- "Self-examination, an honest, hard look at the realities of your existing situation and an in-depth, serious look at how you got to where you are and what your part was in the process."

- A five-step process of maturing: 1) Self-awareness 2) Emotional awareness 3) Emotional maturity 4) Spiritual awareness 5) Spiritual maturity.

- We must face the fear and become 100% responsible for ourselves.

- Many times, we find ourselves in this state because of our lack of self-discipline or a lack of self-denial.

- Emotional awareness - This is where we start to understand and become aware of our emotional states and how we react to emotion, moment by moment.

- The point is not what you do, or what you accomplish, but "who" you are. A taker or giver? A consumer or provider. An idiot or guru?

- Reaching emotional maturity requires us to not only be aware of our emotions and short comings, but to do something with the knowledge. The biggest roadblock to Emotional Maturity is what I call, "Bondage of Self!"

- We must take active responsibility for our thoughts. What is a thought? I believe it is a speculation, an unchecked reason, an unexplored possibility. It's nothing until we analyze it.

- Don't believe everything you think!

- We must learn to recognize where we are on the "emotional curve", every moment of every day.

- We must program our minds to constantly be aware of where we are on the emotional curve whenever a new emotion or thought pops into our minds.

- Arrogance, versus humility, is the battleground of the ego. Our egos can be a destructive force in our lives if they go unnoticed and unchecked.

- "Humility is not thinking less of yourself, humility is thinking about yourself less!"

- Humans are for the most part fear based. You will quickly come to realize most resentments are a result of ego, prejudices, insecurities and fears.

- (Embracing our emotional states). Requires us to stop and think before we act or react. Being able to admit mistakes and work on self-control moment by moment. It requires us to stop, listen, shut up and repeat!

- You will be able to recognize growth when you realize you can finally "observe" without "reacting". It means taking responsibility for your thoughts and analyzing them before reacting. Think before you speak. This confirms you are on the road to emotional maturity.

- Most emotional conflict is a result of frustration created by expectations not being met.

- Spiritual maturity is where we fully realize it's better to be a "giver" than a "taker".

- The most immature way to exist is to be a taker.

- Highest level of maturity? It's what I call, "Looking for A Receiver".

- Here is the FIRST NUGGET: You can't give without receiving. The secret to getting, is giving! Wow! SECOND NUGGET: Be a generous receiver when someone gives something to you. If you don't allow yourself to receive, you're refusing the gifts of others! —and you shut down the flow! Don't do that!

- One of the biggest reasons we fail to mature and heal is our subconscious mind's desire to hold on to our wounds.

- Keeping our wounds alive drains, us of precious energy.

- If you catch yourself looking at every situation from the dark side, you need to eradicate a wound and it starts by eradicating negative self-talk.

- Your subconscious mind believes whatever you tell it. Be careful what you speak and be even more careful what you think!

- Once we come to terms with our own character faults, arrogance, self-pity, victimization, resentments, passive aggressive behavior, always being right, getting even instead of getting ahead, etc., we can start a new quest for enlightenment, a quest for Spiritual Awareness and Self-Actualization.

- I'm talking about an intuition suggesting we do not exist by chance or have just evolved over the last billion years from some natural occurrences/evolution over time.

- This final step in the maturation process runs to infinity, you can never actually reach the goal, as it is ever expanding.

- "Religion is for people who are afraid of going to hell. Spirituality is for people who've been there."

- "When we change our way of thinking, we change". "When we change our hearts, everything changes".

- I now live in peace, serenity and humility due to my new spirituality and The Mind-Body Crossover.

- My spiritual maturity is growing and expanding daily, and I am blessed indeed! As mentioned earlier, (It makes no difference if you are a Hindu, a Buddhist, a Jew, a Christian, a Sikh, a Unitarian, a Muslim, etc.), I encourage you to experience "the spirit", not just religion.

- Then wisdom, spirituality and simplicity manifest in our lives as we learn from the discipline and denial of "standing in the fire".

- We finally realize we are victims of a war we have waged against ourselves!

- We finally realize the opposite of being right is being free!

- Hesitation kills!

ACTION ITEMS: (TELL ME WHAT TO DO)

- Make a list of all your resentments.

- Make a list of the last three times you were wallowing in self-pity, playing the victim, or practicing passive aggressive behavior.

- Make a list of all the excuses you have used.

- List five things you need to stop doing, five things you need to start doing and five things you need to keep doing to take 100% responsibility for what happens in life. Fifteen items total.

CHAPTER THIRTEEN

THE TWO D'S

"Emotional maturity is what you get when you don't get what you want!" What a revealing statement. There are a lot of similar statements and quotes from famous people that substitute the word "Experience" at the beginning of this sentence. I believe Emotional Maturity is more appropriate and is what really starts to happen when we don't get what we want. It's the starting point of the five-step maturity journey mentioned earlier in this book, 1) self-awareness, 2) emotional awareness, 3) emotional maturity, 4) spiritual awareness and 5) the unending quest for spiritual maturity.

Denial and discipline, not desire, shape our lives. These are the Two D's I'm referring to in earlier chapters. Satisfying our desires is an instinct that needs to be monitored and curtailed to make pure progress and advance in life. Most of us don't like to curtail basic desires. We want what we want, want it now, and we usually want MORE! Unfortunately, or should I say fortunately, God does not always see it our way. He has an all-knowing plan which is much higher than the fulfillment of our selfish desires. God tests you because He wants to stretch your faith and build you up not because He wants to beat you down or wear you out! If everything came easy we would not appreciate anything. We must learn that God provides these two axioms, denial and discipline, to help us grow. To help us become ever expanding

"Spiritual Beings". To become winners in the truest sense of the word.

I like to think of it as an attitude adjustment required to make progress in our spiritual growth. It is through giving, sacrifice and being humbled that we start to grow and obtain purpose, passion, joy and fulfillment. This is only accomplished when we fully realize that all good things usually come from sacrifice, and we are required to discipline and deny ourselves to really grow. We must stop thinking about, me, me, me, me, me and start looking for opportunities to help others. As mentioned earlier, the highest form of maturity is "looking for a receiver". Looking for an opportunity to help someone else. This ongoing quest for spiritual maturity by helping others is the Holy Grail to finding peace, serenity and joy. If you seriously want to make a mega-leap in personal growth, you need to address what twelve step program participants call "Bondage of Self". Stop focusing on yourself and start focusing on others! Realize it's not all about you! This requires an emotional leap to a higher plane! It requires humility.

As mentioned, humans are fear-based beings. Fight or flight is a survival technique built into our DNA. As we continue to grow and experience more of life through the aging process we intuitively gain more wisdom if we are paying attention. Wisdom comes to people in different ways, forms, doses and times. I love Emmet Fox's definition: "Wisdom is the perfect blending of intelligence and love".

LOSING IS A LEARNING EXPERIENCE

So often my good intentions do more harm than good. Being a "Helicopter Mom/Dad" feels so right to so many of us, always trying to manipulate every situation to ensure that our children are on the winning team. Winning at all costs! Are you a child of "Helicopter Parents"? I was guilty of this practice from time to time when raising my own children. I wanted the best for them in every aspect and didn't realize the damage I was doing until it was pointed out to me in a gentle way by an astute, emotionally mature, close friend. Fortunately for my kids, I learned this lesson early on and amended my parenting skills immediately. As parents, we often feel a desperate need, to pave the way for our children, but in fact we prevent them from growing through life's real, brutal and necessary terms.

My friend informed me that I might be trying to live my own life through my child's. He suggested this might be due to my own insecurities, and disappointments. This was a hard thing to hear and at first it really "pissed" me off until I took a hard look at the way I was thinking and acting. I also realized the disservice I was doing my children by preventing them from seeing the true, hard realities of life. Not everyone wins all the time! Not everyone, gets their way all the time! Not everyone gets a first-place trophy! Not everyone should get a trophy-period! Not everyone is treated fairly all the time!

The gentleman that helped me realize this deficiency in parenting skills was my coaching partner on my son's Little League team. I noticed he was always encouraging the sons of the opposing team as much as he encouraged our own players. He honestly did not care if his son's team won or not. He was only concerned with lessons learned! I felt like a total idiot when I fully realized, my immature perspective. It was an eye-opening experience that helped jump start my growth to emotional maturity. He eventually became a close friend, confidant and mentor. Today, when I see insecure, immature parents trying to manipulate, teachers, umpires, referees and coaches trying to ensure that their child wins at all costs, I almost get sick at my stomach. There is nothing that hurts your children more. If you catch yourself trying to pave the way for your children as a Helicopter Mom/Dad, you might want to step back and consider if your actions are in the best interest of your children. You are only displaying a huge sign of personal insecurity on your chest! Losing can be one of the most powerful lessons children can ever experience. Let them experience this emotion when you are around to help cope with the feeling. Don't deprive them of this learning experience due to your own insecurity, emotional deficiency or arrogance. As you might expect, losing is also a learning experience for adults.

In the 1960's Michael Mischel, Stanford University psychology researcher, demonstrated how important self-discipline is to success when he conducted what has become known as The Marshmallow Study. He conducted his study by offering a group of young children one marshmallow, Mischel told them that if they could wait for him to return, from running a quick errand to a local store, they could have two marshmallows instead. Pretty challenging for a four-year-old to delay gratification for ten or fifteen minutes. The results were very revealing. Fast forward fourteen years. The children who waited for his return to get an extra marshmallow were more positive, self-motivating, persistent in the face of difficulties and able to delay gratification in pursuit of their personal goals. They had developed the habit of a successful adult. The habit of delayed gratification points to greater career/job satisfaction which leads to higher incomes, more thriving marriages and better overall general health.

The children who did not wait were more demanding, troubled, disturbed, indecisive, mistrustful, less self-confident and appeared to have an entitlement attitude. They were still incapable of delaying instant gratification. Even more troubling, these kids scored an average of 210 points less on SAT tests. Why? Distraction and the desire for instant gratification got in the way of good focused study time. If not addressed, lack of impulse control will continue to trip these kids up throughout life. This can result in poor job performance, bad marriages, low income, bad health and all-around exasperation and frustration with life in general.

If you have a one-marshmallow kind of kid, don't give up! Thank God. Delayed gratification can be learned. Use leisure time to teach this skill. You can choose books and toys and that reinforce self-discipline and reward the behaviors daily. Reinforcing desired behaviors when children are young and open to new concepts is far easier than trying to change behavior when they are older.

Once we recognize the importance of denial and discipline, we have an opportunity to view life in a different way, free of the total dominance of our out of control, unchecked egos. It is a powerful and necessary ingredient for obtaining emotional maturity and very important for our ongoing and never-ending quest for spiritual maturity. Knowing that success requires these two axioms in healthy doses prepare us for the tough, real battles presented by life. It gets us ready to accept the fact that life is filled with challenges meant to help us grow and mature. It is also imperative for us to instill these values in children. Stop trying to "fix" everything for your children!

I/We also need to stop trying to fix everything for everyone else in our lives: our spouses, employees, friends, significant others, etc. My basic instinct is to impart so-called "wisdom" to anyone and everyone, as I'm absolutely convinced that I'm so smart, brilliant and intuitive! BS! BS! BS! I/We must realize that nobody is asking for our solution. No one is asking to be fixed. I need to stop trying to fix others! I finally realize that I need to focus on shutting up, listening and fixing myself!

The biggest benefit of embracing the Two D's is that it provides a pathway for us to love ourselves in a healthy, nonjudgmental way. Focus on this one: "Things will come to you if you stop reaching for them". Something I need to be reminded of daily. You probably noticed a lot of self-deprecation where I say, I must have "BUMPED MY HEAD". Obviously, that's not a very healthy attitude if overdone. It also can be perceived, a smart-ass way for me to say, "Hey look at me, I can make fun of myself, aren't I cool?" I recently read a book or article by Richard Rohr where he made an interesting statement (paraphrase), "Self-deprecation is just as self-centered as self-inflation." After much consideration, I believe he is right. I learned a lot by internalizing this statement regarding self-deprecation. From this point on in my life I vow to only speak positive words over myself and my performance. I encourage you to do the same for yourself and loved ones, especially your children.

One last comment about self-esteem and self-deprecation. Sometimes we are just too hard on ourselves and don't give enough credit for our emotional maturity. A mentor and close friend, Jim Spivey, brought this to my attention one night over dinner. He labeled his theory "The Always". It basically says that sometimes we have already accomplished something or that we already are what we are striving to become, but we just don't see or believe it as fact. We don't give ourselves proper credit. Kind of like a scotoma. We misinterpret our own consciousness/essence. Here is Jim's quote:

> "Inside each of us is a core BEING, a pure ESSENCE that has ALWAYS been TRUE. It often communicates to us through dreams and visions, when we take the time to dive into our own depths

beneath the surface noise of our lives and the part of us caught up in frenzied response, identifying with that unconscious response, that part that misinterprets glimpses of our core as what we want to be and must work hard to become, while afraid we'll never get there".

At the end of this book you will see a Life Plan that Jim helped create as a dissertation/statement about me, labeled, "Who I Am". He is a talented mentor who has challenged me and changed my life for the better, by helping me grow and realize my own self-worth. He has created hundreds of Life Plans for his mentees. See "About the Author" at the end of this book.

To summarize, it all starts with recognizing the absolute power of implementing denial and discipline into our daily life on an ongoing and never-ending basis. It requires Humility, "A clear recognition and acceptance of who I really am, followed by a sincere attempt to become what I could be". A winner is born when we fully surrender our egos and embrace love as a way of living. We must give up our old selfish ways and start helping others with an attitude of love. We must give it (love) away to keep it. Our identity as winners isn't destroyed by surrender, its strengthened. Our identity as winners isn't destroyed by adversity or denial and discipline, it strengthened. The power of the universe is unleashed at the point of our greatest defeats and weakness. In other words, pain is the touchstone of progress! Greatness and progress demand surrender, total surrender. "When I am weak, then I am strong." (2 Corinthians 12:10).

CHAPTER SUMMARY

 GOLDEN NUGGETS:

- "Emotional maturity is what you get when you don't get what you want!"

- Denial and discipline, not desire shape our lives.

- God tests you because He wants to stretch your faith and build you up—not because he wants to beat you down or wear you out!

- If you seriously want to make a mega-leap in your personal growth, you need to address, what twelve step program participants call "Bondage of Self". Stop focusing on yourself and start focusing on others! Realize it's not all about you! This requires an emotional leap to a higher plane!

- Losing can be one of the most powerful lessons you and your children can ever experience. Let your children experience this emotion when you are around to help cope with the feeling.

- Once we recognize the importance of denial and discipline we have an opportunity to view life in a different way, free of the total dominance of our out of control, unchecked egos.

- It gets us ready to accept the fact that life is filled with challenges that are meant to help us grow and mature.

- It requires, HUMILITY: "A clear recognition and acceptance of who I really am, followed by a sincere attempt to become what I could be".

- "Self-deprecation is just as self-centered as self-inflation!"

- In other words, pain is the touchstone of progress!

- Hesitation kills!

ACTION ITEMS: (TELL ME WHAT TO DO)

- Start looking for a "receiver" every day. Help someone in some small way every day for the rest of your life and put a reminder on your calendar.

- Make a list of things that need discipline or denial in your life.

- Make a vow and write it in your journal to stop all self-deprecation today.

The Two D's

CHAPTER FOURTEEN

SUCCESSFUL ENTREPRENEURS AND CHANGE

What is the secret to be a successful entrepreneur? I've spent years interviewing successful people about what they thought was the most critical attribute needed for success. Many of the people I interviewed, some very wealthy and successful, have a hard time identifying the major key(s) to their own success. I get a lot of the standard answers one would expect such as hard work, being your own person, being in the right place at the right time, not afraid to take a chance, listening to your gut, etc. Regardless, it was difficult to identify any one key factor or secret to success that all entrepreneurs used to achieve that success.

After my move to Houston in 1975, I spent some serious time trying to figure out what I wanted to do with my life and career. I knew one thing for sure! I was looking for employment that did not limit my financial earning capability. I thought of myself as an entrepreneur and wanted to have the freedom to make a lot of money and basically be my own boss. I talked with many people and interviewed for a lot of different jobs trying to find a good fit for my desires and my personality. After several false starts, I eventually ended up in what I thought was the perfect position, working in the commercial real estate business for the preeminent firm in Houston, The Horne Company. It was a stroke of luck and a good fit! I was determined to be successful and worked like a maniac to make it big.

I was lucky early on in this business and the industry allowed me to make unlimited compensation. In 1982, I generated a $67,000,000 investment transaction in Midland with the Horne Company and thought I had hit the big time. This was considered a monster deal in the early eighties and commissions on these types of transactions were considerably higher than they are today. All the hard work around this transaction was accomplished by a good friend, A. Richard Wilson, an investment broker with The Horne Company, to whom I referred the business. We ended up selling eight mid-rise office buildings which was one of the largest transactions in the commercial real estate industry in 1983. Richard negotiated a very lucrative commission on this transaction and it was a substantial payday for both of us. I learned a lot about the art of negotiation from Richard on this transaction and it has served me well over the years.

This early success encouraged me to dig harder and find out more about what made other people successful, as I wanted to duplicate my efforts to ensure extraordinary financial success. In my quest for financial freedom I discovered something much more valuable that has helped in numerous other ways as well. Another addition to, and expansion of, The Mind-Body Crossover.

After my mental and physical transformation in 1976, I was more than curious, about what had happened to me, and how I could lose weight, stop smoking, stop drinking and run a marathon in a span of eight short months. Prior to the transformation I spent a considerable amount of my time expanding my knowledge of:

- The Mind-Body Crossover
- Future Pacing
- The Countdown

- The power of the subconscious
- Goal setting
- Creative visualization
- The psychology of "change"
- The power of repetition
- The constructs of habit formation

The study of these subjects helped me further define my personality and entrepreneurial tendencies. I was very curious about how successful entrepreneurs thought, acted and reacted. I was talking to a lot of people, trying to figure out the key to be a successful entrepreneur.

In the mid 1990's I had the privilege of interviewing Doug Sanders, golf's colorful ambassador, and eventually became friends with one of the greatest golfers of all time. I met Doug in 1998 when a friend took me to see his impressive golf memorabilia collection. Doug has since become a person I admire from a story-telling perspective. Being a good, or should I say a great, storyteller is an invaluable attribute. Doug recently shared a funny story about how important it is to have an advantage whenever you have an opportunity to make a bet. Even the slightest edge can sometimes mean the difference between losing and winning. He shared how he used to carry bogus wooden golf tees in his bag when playing a casual round of golf with friends when wagering. The wooden tees were altered by shaving off a sixteenth of an inch on the top to prevent the tee from properly holding a ball. In other words, it's impossible to tee the ball as the top of the tee is flat and the ball keeps falling/rolling off! It's hilarious to slip one of these tees to your friends when you are making a wager and see the frustration when they can't tee the ball. Gives you a very slight advantage as the "Mark" is flustered once you reveal the joke.

Remember when Lee Trevino pulled out a very authentic looking rubber rattlesnake and threw it at Jack Nicklaus before the playoff in a PGA Tournament?

I recently spent several years helping Doug try to find a location for a restaurant concept he had to display his large collection of golf memorabilia. Doug is a guy who taught me a lot about success, a lot about "the hustle", and a lot about practice, practice, practice. I recently had lunch with Doug to talk about his ideas on success. He was quick to point out that he thinks all great winners have several things many of us have but are not willing to undertake to become successful. Here is what he shared regarding winners and successful people:

1.) They know they have talent., i.e. they are confident.

2.) They are willing to take a risk.

3.) They practice their trade a lot. Practice. Practice. Practice.

4.) They are always looking for an opportunity and/or advantage.

Doug recently turned 83 and still believes number three above, practice, is the most important. He still jogs every day and does about two hundred full body sit ups, five days a week. And he still hits a lot of golf balls every week. Practice. Practice. Practice!

Doug loves to compete and is notorious for his betting prowess on the golf course. He co-authored a book: <u>Doug Sanders – Action on the First Tee, 130 Different Ways to Make a Bet.</u> I encourage buying it if you enjoy making wagers on the golf course.

P.S. I'm convinced that Doug's secret motto is: never make a bet unless you are 99 to 100% sure you are going to win! A great attribute for an astute businessman as well.

Here is a quick story demonstrating how this might work: "The Mark" is usually taken to the cleaners several times by this type of trick before he finally realizes what is happening to him. The Shark approaches The Mark with a seemingly straight forward bet The Mark feels certain he can win. "Gary, my boy, --You got a C Note on ya?" says, The Shark. A wager is coming. Not being one to shy away from an opportunity to make a quick $100, The Mark confirms that he does indeed have a C note in his possession. The Shark points to a tall, skinny pine tree about 50 to 75 yards across the course on the other side of the first tee from where they are standing. The Shark has five golf balls in his hand and lays them in a row in front of The Mark. He proceeds to bet that he can hit that pine tree with at least one of the five golf balls. (5 balls-The Setup). The Mark immediately starts laughing and says anybody could hit that tree, as it had a limb span of at least twenty feet and even a novice could hit it with five tries. The Shark stops The Mark in mid-sentence, proceeding to say he meant hitting the trunk of the tree, which is only about 24 inches wide and about four feet high. (The Second Setup). That changes everything. Sensing an opportunity to make a quick $100 and thinking of himself as a shrewd negotiator, The Mark quickly offers to accept the bet, but only gives him three tries instead of five. The Mark, is surprised when The Shark rather quickly accepts the challenge with the reduced number of balls. The Mark, thinking this is no easy feat, feels confident that The Shark can't hit the trunk unless he gets extremely lucky as it is a long shot of at least 50 yards, and the trunk is not very wide.

They shake hands on the bet and The Shark stands over the three balls. He looks at the tree one time and swings at the first ball, hitting the tree square in the middle of the trunk. The Mark is pissed to say the least but is even more shocked at what happens next. Without looking up, The Shark continues to swing and hits the second and third ball without looking up! All three hit the trunk in a matter of about six seconds total, as The Shark never stops swinging. Little does The Mark know the fix was in!! Later, The Mark finally realizes The Shark has probably been practicing that kind of shot just about every day of his life. The chances of him missing the trunk three times is absolutely zero.

Wow! Whenever a wager looks like a sure thing, rest assured a fix is in and you are about to lose money. An even better lesson is to be aware that whenever anything, especially a business deal, looks too good to be true, it's probably not! Get rich quick claims always have a fix! Be aware!

P.S. I'm not sure, but I think The Shark in this description was Doug Sanders and yours truly was The Mark! Not positive, but I am missing a "C" Note! Go figure!

CHANGE

I continued to interview highly successful entrepreneurs on a regular basis. Early in this process, I learned a very valuable lesson about "change" that I think is worthy of mention. Most people hate change. In the mid 1980's I finally met a unique entrepreneur who gave me some valuable insight to success that was a real game-changer for me. His name was John Sage, a local real estate developer and successful entrepreneur. He had a very intriguing story and is one of the few people I ever met that was a highly successful secular entrepreneur, social entrepreneur and spiritual entrepreneur. Needless-to-say, I have never met a person who was so successful in three different areas. He shared with me a key secret to success that he used in all three of these fields. Take heed, as it is very powerful secret and can help you make mega leaps in every area of your life!

I met John through my brother-in-law, Don Tallman, who was John's CPA/Accountant. During the late seventies and early eighties, John was a successful real estate developer and invested in tax shelters where investors were reaping considerable returns due to several deductions that allowed 3 to 1 write offs in some cases, and many people were taking advantage of these write offs. The government eventually repealed/changed the interpretation of the rule and many were forced to recapture income due to the government change. Many people, John included were hit with massive tax liabilities. Needless-to-say, this put a huge financial burden on investors, forcing many out of business and some into bankruptcy. John, being a highly successful and determined businessman, fought his way back after this devastating setback, that took years to rectify. He was a highly successful secular entrepreneur.

A horrible event occurred in 1993, changing John's life forever, and causing him to become a highly successful, social entrepreneur. His sister was tragically and brutally murdered randomly in her home. The two individuals were running from police and looking for a car to steal. They happened upon Johns' sister, Marilyn, and brutally stabbed her numerous times and then placed a plastic bag over her head. She died from the brutal stab wounds and suffocation. John was very close to his sister and was emotionally devastated by her death. He was obsessed with finding who killed her. He spent every moment helping to track down, prosecute and incarcerate the man and woman responsible. Johns rage over this incident emotionally affected every fiber of his being, but he eventually sought help to overcome his grief and forgive the two perpetrators.

A healing process ensued that eventually led John to form one of the most highly rated and successful prison ministries in the country. His prison ministry, Bridges to Life is focused on helping victims and families of victims, deal with grief. I personally worked in the ministry for several years and can attest to it's phenomenal success. The ministry brings perpetrators together with victims to facilitate the healing process. A powerful ministry! It has received numerous commendations and recognition all over the country. His work inside the prison system, at both state and county levels along with the success of the ministry, made him a highly successful social entrepreneur. In addition to the United States, today the ministry is also operating in four foreign countries.

In 2001, John's family suffered another tragic, life changing event when his son John Jr. was critically injured in a snow skiing accident, leaving him a paraplegic. John and his wife Frances faced this tragedy head on and started an internet prayer chain requesting prayer to help save their son during his critical recovery. Today, John's son is leading a productive life. John's Christian faith in a higher power and persistence against insurmountable odds makes him a notable spiritual entrepreneur in addition to the two already mentioned.

I want to share a secret with you about this story. Put it in your memory bank, as it is very powerful. If you implement it, the secret can bring you money, happiness and joy. Very powerful!

Here is the secret! Hopefully, we will not have to face the kind of tragedies related in these three stories, but there is a great lesson to be learned. Curious about how John survived these tragic events, I asked him to consider the key factor that allowed him and other successful entrepreneurs to overcome adversity and still succeed. I got a call several weeks later. John relayed the one thread he saw through these events. He noted that each was precipitated by change, "massive change." He told me something very insightful. He said the number one thing he thinks most success entrepreneurs know, and act on, is related to one important fact. He said, we all instinctively hate change. Highly successful entrepreneurs know, more than anyone, that there is only one thing in the world that never changes, and that is "Change." He believes the key is that highly successful people accept immediately that "change" has occurred and intuitively comprehend that it cannot be reversed. They act and capitalize on it, while everyone else sits around and gripes and complains about the change and does not take any action. Action is key! By taking immediate action, the highly successful person makes mega leaps over the catastrophe and competition. Don't forget this little jewel of wisdom which used properly, can help you make a lot of money, make mega leaps over the competition and advance your career exponentially.

I have continued to interview and talk with numerous highly successful individuals from all walks of life, hoping to find what makes them tick. Obviously, there are numerous factors contributing to success, but we must be vigilant and astute to learn from others if we hope to be successful ourselves. Always be inquisitive about the success of others if you want to experience the same success in your own career.

This discussion on "Change" reminds me of a funny but very poignant and insightful observation about three (3) frogs sitting on a log besides a pond contemplating jumping into the water. All the frogs seem to be "willing" to jump into the water. Finally, one of the frogs make a "decision" to jump in. How many frogs are left on the log? The answer is three! Being willing and making a decision to act, are only two thirds of the process. You must take "action" and actually jump in the water if you want to be successful. Never forget that manifesting "Change" is a three-part process. Willingness, decision and action! Action is the key and the most important. It starts by asking yourself if you are willing to change. Are you fed up with your existing circumstances enough to acknowledge willingness? Then you must make a definitive decision to change. Next you actually make the plunge! The Countdown is the secret to manifesting the change you desire and plunge into an exciting and fulfilling future. This requires you to get out of your comfort zone and act! Take the plunge!

CHAPTER SUMMARY

 GOLDEN NUGGETS:

- Highly successful entrepreneurs never make a bet unless they are 99 to 100% sure they are going to win!

- Whenever a wager looks like a sure thing, rest assured a "fix" is in and you are about to lose money.

- An even better lesson is to be aware that whenever anything, especially a business deal, looks too good to be true, it's probably not! Get rich quick claims always have a fix! Be aware!

- We all instinctively hate "Change".

- Highly successful entrepreneurs know, more than anyone else, there is only one thing in the world that never changes, "Change."

- Highly Successful people accept immediately that "Change" has occurred and intuitively comprehend, it cannot be reversed. They act and capitalize on it while everyone else sits around griping and complaining about the "Change".

- Dealing with "Change". Action is key! By taking immediate action, the highly successful person makes mega leaps over the catastrophe and competition.

- Always be inquisitive about the success of others if you want to experience it in your own career.

- Hesitation kills!

ACTION ITEMS: (TELL ME WHAT TO DO)

- Where in your memory bank have you been lax in looking realistically at a deal you knew was bogus, pursuing it anyway and getting burned. Write it in the margin of this page.

- Write in the margin a situation where you failed to act and missed out on a windfall.

CHAPTER FIFTEEN

POWER OF: TEACH TO LEARN & MENTORING

In 1994, I inadvertently stumbled upon a concept on how to build a strategic plan for your life, that has become a part of my training. It's a simple concept, that's been around for years and taught by many educators. It involves the learning process and how we help and teach ourselves as we help and teach others. The basic premise is that when we teach someone a new skill it forces us to enhance our skill level in the process.

I came to realize the concept's real power in 1994 when my fourteen-year-old son Matthew wanted to learn tennis as a freshman at Dulles High School in Sugar Land. I played on the tennis team in high school and college, never wanting to be one of those fathers who pushed their kids to participate in my sport of choice. I don't think Matt even knew at the time that I played the sport competitively, but I was excited when he asked me to teach him. His goal was to try out for the team at Dulles, one of the largest Five A schools in the state and very competitive. Secretly, I was skeptical at best about his prospects, as I had seen the team practicing on numerous occasions from our home across the street from Dulles. They were excellent players, excellent athletes and very competitive.

Matt was super determined, but I didn't think he had the foot speed to compete with Class Five A singles tennis players. We attacked the courts and learned the basics, practicing and working on foot speed drills relentlessly. He surprised me by being a quick study with a natural tennis stroke that served him well in the sport. He still plays competitively today at thirty-seven.

During 1994, I was on an airplane almost every day and could not practice with him much during the week. I realized he would never make it without an extraordinary amount of court time and additional training, so I approached the country club tennis pro about giving Matt private lessons. They were expensive, but I felt it was the only way for him to get the needed instruction and court time. The pro fortunately had several openings and we signed Matt up for lessons twice a week. The pro mentioned he was looking for someone to help teach his 4-year-old class and was interested to find out if Matt had the skill level and knowledge of the game to be a part-time coach for these young kids. He didn't really have the skill level, but I said he did! I told him Matt would be at his office the following Monday to start his own lessons and be available to start helping with the four-year-old kids who were learning to play for the first time. It turns out Matt made enough money teaching kids to more than pay for his own private lessons with money to spare. One heck of a deal, as I had also been encouraging Matt to get a part time summer job from a responsibility standpoint. I thought summer jobs were educational and beneficial, as I always worked as a kid and it taught me a lot about discipline and denial. Wow, two birds with one stone.

Matt was ecstatic when I told him I had set up private lessons at the country club. However, he freaked out when I told him about the part time coaching job for the four-year old's. "Dad there is no way I can do that! I just started playing a couple of months ago, and I don't know how to teach someone else!" I didn't flinch. I told him we had several weeks before his first lesson and I would teach him some basic training drills and he would be OK. He was scared to death but went ahead anyway and became a real hit almost immediately with the young kids.

Matt did not make the tennis team his freshman year, but he practiced and learned a lot about the strategic part of the game helping make up for his lack of foot speed. His sophomore year he tried out again and claimed one of the alternate positions but didn't play that much. He did however, continue to teach at the country club and became a good instructor. He gained a lot of personal confidence, by teaching young kids and his skills continued to progress at an exponential rate. His Junior year he made the team and his technique, strategic knowledge and foot speed increased measurably. He was very competitive and played doubles and some singles. His progression surprised me.

The story takes a phenomenal turn his senior year as Matt wins one of the singles slots and is beating almost everyone he plays in numerous citywide tournaments. Then the unimaginable happens! He attends the John Newcome statewide tennis tournament in the Texas Hill Country and wins the State Grand Prix Tennis Championship, beating every other Five A singles player from Dallas, Fort Worth, San Antonio, El Paso, Austin, etc. He never lost a single set. Fortunately, I attended the tournament and recorded the entire state event and have every game on film. The "proud father" no doubt!

Matt told me years later how scared he was of making a fool of himself teaching those young kids. He was determined to learn everything he could about tennis in those two weeks before he started teaching, forcing him to make a mega leap. An agreement to teach someone else a new skill forces you to "up" your own level of skill. A very powerful lesson. If you desire to excel at something, sign up to teach others!

"No one learns as much about a subject as one who is forced to teach it." — Peter F. Drucker

MENTORSHIP

"Mentorship is a relationship in which a more experienced or more knowledgeable person helps to guide a less experienced or less knowledgeable person".

Matt learned a lot more than just tennis from the pro at the country club. Outside of me, his dad, this was his first experience with a mentor. The pro taught him a lot about living and dealing with human emotion. Parents of the kids at the country club, who pay for private tutoring or tennis lessons, can be very demanding and extremely arrogant. Matt got an irreplaceable education on dealing with some very emotionally immature and difficult parents during his stint as a tennis coach for four-year-old's at the country club. The pro taught him a lot about human interaction. A great mentor.

I can't stress enough the importance of mentoring, as I grew up in an era where mentoring was almost nonexistent. We usually gained some informal mentoring from teachers or coaches in school, but it was not something we were taught to seek out and pursue.

FAST TRACK TO FINDING GREAT MENTORS

Here is my best advice on finding great mentors. I encourage all my students to find multiple mentors. Having three or four formal mentors, would be the best of all worlds and here's how it works. I require my mentees to interview the most influential people in the industry, hoping to convince a highly successful and influential person to mentor them. For example, if you are a recent college graduate with a degree in engineering and want to get in the oil and gas business, don't settle for interviewing an executive vice president of a mid-size oil and gas company. Call the CEO of Exxon, Chevron or Shell Oil, instead! Go straight to the top. This requires a lot of nerve and a tremendous amount of preparation and networking for the young entrepreneur just starting his career.   Most highly successful people are usually willing to talk with young people and it is their way of giving back. It's the prospective mentee's responsibility to have fifteen great questions to ask once they get the interview. It's best to attempt this right out of college or very early in your career, as the younger you are the more likely you are to get in to see "The Big Dog".

Remember, you are the one conducting the interview, not the CEO. You are the one asking the questions, not the CEO. You are not in his office groveling for a job. You want to know how he became successful, how he became the CEO, how he climbed to the top, what he thinks is important for the young guy starting out, etc. (These are some of the fifteen questions you should be asking).

This astute technique allows you to hold all the power in this situation. You are asking the questions, not her/him. If successful in getting a meeting and performing well during your interview, there is a high chance of you getting a job offer from the CEO, which is a lot more meaningful than getting an offer from the Director of Human Resources. Regardless of the outcome, be sure to ask the most powerful question on your way out of his office. "Who do you know who......?" These are the five most powerful words for any great salesman and can generate another fifteen questions almost immediately for the astute interviewer. One question might be: Who do you know who---might be looking for someone with my qualifications? Who do you know who----I might be able to interview to gain more knowledge about this profession? Who do you know who----might be willing to mentor me? This is the best way I know to find power mentors. Even if the CEO does not have a job for you he/she might be willing to mentor you. Very powerful.

Below are some of my favorite quotes regarding mentoring and mentorship:

> "Tell me and I forget, teach me and I may remember, involve me and I learn." - Benjamin Franklin

> "It is a solemn duty to change lives positively. It is a noble honor to inspire and be there for others. It is an irresistible necessity to have empathy; to understand the situations and the reasons for the actions of others. Real mentoring is less of neither the candid smile nor the amicable friendship that exists between the mentor and the mentee and much more of the impacts. The indelible great footprints the mentor lives on the mind of the mentee in a life changing way. How the mentor changes the mentee from ordinariness to extra-ordinariness; the seed of purposefulness that is planted and nurtured for great fruits; the prayer from afar from the mentor to the mentee; and the great inspirations the mentee takes from the mentor to dare unrelentingly to face the storms regardless of how arduous the errand may be with or without the presence of the mentor" - Ernest Agyemang Yeboah

> "What you leave behind is not what is engraved in stone monuments, but what is woven into the lives of others." — Pericles, 495-429 BC, prominent

and influential Greek statesman, orator, and general of Athens.

Remember this one: "Mentors are just as important as credentials."

"Remember that mentor leadership is all about serving. Jesus said, "For even the Son of Man came not to be served but to serve others and to give his life as a ransom for many" (Mark 10:45)."
- <u>Tony Dungy</u>, <u>The Mentor Leader: Secrets to Building People and Teams That Win Consistently</u>

Another one of my favorites comes from my business partner, mentor and great friend Gregg Raymond:

"My Life's Mission: If it's wrong don't do it. If it's right do it with joy, enthusiasm and accountability. Stay close to Christ. Enjoy the ride".

CHAPTER SUMMARY

⚛ GOLDEN NUGGETS:

- When we teach someone a new skill, it forces us to enhance our skill in the process.

- Once you agree to teach someone a new skill, it forces you to "up" your own level.

- "No one learns as much about a subject as one who is forced to teach it." — Peter F. Drucker

- "Mentors are just as important as credentials."

- "Tell me and I forget, teach me and I may remember, involve me and I learn." -Benjamin Franklin

- If you graduate with a degree in engineering and want to get in the oil and gas business, don't settle for interviewing an executive vice president of a mid-size oil and gas company. Call the CEO of Exxon, Chevron or Shell Oil, instead. Go straight to the top.

- Remember, you are the one conducting the interview, not the CEO. You are the one asking the questions, not the CEO. You are not in his office groveling for a job.

- The most powerful question any salesman can ask: "Who do you know who......?"

- Hesitation kills!

ACTION ITEMS: (TELL ME WHAT TO DO)

- Make a list of the ten most influential people in your city and use creativity to land an appointment to interview them about their success.

- List the fifteen questions you plan to ask during the interview.

- Set a deadline on your calendar to acquire a minimum of three mentors, using the technique in this chapter, by a specified date. Deadlines are very important. Taking massive action is just as important.

CHAPTER SIXTEEN

THE THREE P'S

This short chapter is about high-performance individuals and how they stay on top of their game for the long haul without giving up and/or burning out. I learned this valuable lesson from Rick McCord, a highly successful entrepreneur, friend, mentor, Christian and real estate developer in Houston who recently died after living a life filled with joy, passion and success. He had a true "compass setting" for living life to its fullest. The Three P's represent three words he used to give balance, focus and direction to his life. A unique concept that teaches a lot about high-performance living and high-performance individuals.

I got to know Rick on a personal level during several trips to South Dakota to hunt pheasant. I was working for a large janitorial maintenance company in 1998, heading up sales and marketing and we often took clients/potential clients on hunting and fishing trips to build rapport and expand relationships. Rick owned several large office buildings and we were constantly trying to expand our commercial cleaning business with his organization. Rick was a valued client who had a flair for marketing and sales in his own business and we were "Two Peas in Pod" when it came to marketing, sales and building relationships. He had my "number" early on and used to call me the "King of Embellishment"! Fortunately for me that was a term of endearment coming from Rick, even though it certainly came with a touch of sarcasm embedded in the statement. He loved to give me as much "grief" as possible when we were together. We had a lot of fun kidding each other about the art of "BS".

I was always impressed with his success and interviewed him early-on in my discovery process to learn his secret to success as a high-performance entrepreneur. Over the years, when I would try to contact him, he always seemed to be on vacation. I would call his assistant Mary and invariably she would tell me Rick is in Central America or Canada. However, when I inquired about his whereabouts she never really said he was on vacation, just out of the office. He just happened to be in some exotic location like Belize or the Seychelles Islands. In fact, he was practicing what he called The Third P.

On a flight to South Dakota he told me about the Three P's. Explaining that he separated his business life into three types of actions, all starting with the letter P. He claimed that all business success required attention to what he called the Three P's.

THE FIRST P

Every time he attempted a new undertaking, regardless of its composition, i.e. building a new building, starting a new company, etc. he would spend an inordinate amount of time in Preparation, what he called The First P. To Rick, it made no difference if you were attempting something large or small, significant or insignificant, preparing to build a massive office building, meeting with bankers for a loan or going on an initial sales call. He believed that all success started with investigation and extensive preparation for the event or undertaking. He was an astute observer of people, understood personalities of most everyone around him and used it to his benefit. He was rarely, if ever, unprepared for anything!

THE SECOND P

The second action step involved performance. Rick was always highly focused on Performance and spent an inordinate amount of time getting ready for his own performance. He explained that whenever he was meeting with lenders or investors, he had orchestrated in his own mind exactly how an event would take place long before the actual meeting. He visualized the outcome which required a lot of thought and role playing to pull off in a winning fashion. He also was very demanding of the performance of those he hired to do a job.

THE THIRD P

The third action step was the most interesting and revealing. He quizzed me if I had any idea what the last P word might be. Wow, I was unable to get this one. I made about six guesses before giving up. To my surprise, The Third P was Play! Wow, what a concept. He claimed that his creativity was released in the third action. He believed that it was necessary to relax and totally "unplug". To get away, rest and restore. Rick owned a private one-acre island on the Lake of the Woods in Ontario, Canada that he used as a place of solitude, restoration and recharging. There were only limited electronics at his second home by design. No TV etc. He noted that play included and demanded a lot of "quiet" time.

Rick always believed you never stop growing. From self-awareness to an unending quest for spiritual maturity, he never stopped growing and expanding. He seemed to be at the investigative forefront of anything new, always willing to grow and embrace new ideas. This trait continued into his later years. The first ten years of our relationship were focused totally on business and he was driven to keep McCord Development as the industry leader. Being an emotionally mature individual, who understood human interaction better than most, was probably one of the reasons he was so successful as a businessman. The last 10 years showed another aspect of Rick as he continued to grow toward spiritual maturity. A transformation in belief system caused him to embrace Christianity in a much bigger way the last 10 year of his life and he carried that message to employees and McCord Development in general.

What did I learn from Rick? Work, work, work can be a bad habit to acquire. So many of us think it's magnanimous to work more than anyone else in the office, put in the most hours, forgo vacations, etc. Big mistake! Your creativity will nose dive. Highly successful entrepreneurs are open to new ideas and new ways of growth. They know the value of the "Play" secret when it comes to creativity and foregoing burn out! Play, Play, Play - interesting concept to embrace! A high-value activity, for the person searching for significance, purpose and success.

CHAPTER SUMMARY

⚜ GOLDEN NUGGETS:

- Work, work, work can be a bad habit to acquire.

- The Three P's represent three words used to give balance, focus and direction to life.

- He claimed that all business success required attention to "the Three P's."

- First P - All success starts with investigation and extensive Preparation for the event or undertaking.

- Second P - He was always highly focused on Performance and spent an inordinate amount of time getting ready for his own performance.

- Third P - To my surprise, the Third P is Play!

- He claimed that his creativity was released in the third action. (Play).

- Play, Play, Play - interesting concept to embrace! A high-value activity, for the person searching for significance, purpose and success.

- Hesitation kills!

ACTION ITEMS: (TELL ME WHAT TO DO)

- On your calendar schedule four (4) short mini vacations, one for each quarter of the year where you can unplug and rejuvenate.

- Identify your favorite quiet place, where you go to unplug and rejuvenate. Where you can be alone to pray, meditate and not be interrupted. Schedule calendar dates and visit it often.

CHAPTER SEVENTEEN

SURRENDER AND HOPE APPEAR

Where are you in your life's journey? Are you OK with your accomplishments, direction and current condition? Your ethics? Your morals? Are you happy, joyous and free? Are you experiencing a tremendous amount of joy? Are you all that you ever hoped you would be? Has "The Teacher" shown up yet in your life?

If you would have asked me these questions five years ago, the response would have been negative, depressing, hopeless and sad. I was still living inside my addiction. My life looked like a train wreck! I was a full-blown addict, thinking that life was over and refusing to get help! Refusing to surrender. Refusing to cry "uncle"!

My career was in shambles. I had lost three profitable businesses due to my addiction and refusal to surrender. I owed the IRS a tremendous amount of money due to some unscrupulous partners, and I was heading towards divorce like a freight train. I was narcissistic, stubborn and hopeless! I was refusing to live life on life's terms and I was blaming everyone but myself for my predicament. I was thoroughly convinced that life without alcohol was boring and no fun and not worth living.

Today, that has all changed 180 degrees. Today I'm free of the IRS and back in the black financially with more opportunities than ever from a business perspective and growing towards

Spiritual Maturity from a personal perspective. I've taken a 100% responsibility for what happens to me from this point forward. I've given up the pity party and the victimization and finally realized that no one is going to help me but me!

Coincidentally, I'm using the same road map to recover from this horrific downfall that I used to acquire my original success thirty-five years ago. The process for building a strategic plan for your life, described in this book, works regardless of your personal situation, dilemmas and age. All that's required is discipline, denial and surrender. Surprisingly this can be a lot of fun!

Today, I'm having more fun sober than I ever thought possible! I never realized what I was missing. I joined a twelve-step program over five years ago, and my life has never been the same. I've embraced my recovery program and found a whole new way of living filled with passion and purpose. I never realized the power of twelve step programs until I immersed myself in one. Rehabilitation was nothing like I expected. In fact, it was totally opposite of what I thought. A true diamond in the rough! The whole premise of rehabilitation for me is centered around giving to others and getting out of my ego and bondage to self. There are hundreds of rehab programs that address every possible addiction, and most are highly successful when implemented properly and seriously with proper support.

However, dealing with addiction is a unique undertaking! Alcoholism is a disease. Once understood you can treat it as such and start to recover. Dealing with addiction requires surrender. What an interesting word! I've learned that by surrendering I've joined the winning team. After my downfall and financial collapse, I finally cried "uncle". I had hit my bottom and could not continue to live in my addiction. I was tired and beat up, convinced there was a better way to live and determined to find it! I finally surrendered and sought help. I decided I did not want to live in my addiction any longer. I could see the value and benefit of every mistake I had made in the past. I could use this knowledge to secure my recovery and adopted a whole new way of living, a whole new set of values and a whole new set of words that defined the new me. Words like forgiveness, hope, generosity, altruism, peace, compassion, gratefulness, humility, kindness, integrity, love and joy. Quite different from Sex, Drugs, Rock-N-Roll and MORE! Forgiveness was at the top of my list. I should say self-forgiveness. It wasn't until I forgave myself that I can forgive others and get out of Bondage of Self.

"Your destiny is shaped by the quality of your personal relationships!". I coined this phrase several years ago, upon realizing my recovery was a result of the altruism of others in my life. The connection to other people helped me to grow and mature. Once I acquiesced, so many people gave to me without expecting anything in return, the true definition of altruism.

I've come to realize that all human beings are fear based and we are all wounded. We all grow through pain and tough situations. If we want our wounds to heal, we must help others to heal. We must learn to give without expectation. This requires intimate connection and vulnerability with other human beings. It's not a private journey - Our lives were meant to connect with others. I often practice connecting with others through witnessing. Whenever I'm eating at a restaurant with my better half, Babs, we attempt to connect with others through prayer. When the waitress/waiter brings our food, we tell them we are getting ready to pray over our food and ask them if there is anything we can pray for on their behalf. We find this approach to be non-confrontational and spiritually very rewarding. One young waitress stopped serving immediately and got on her knees and held our hands when Babs asked the question. Very humbling. To stay connected with others, I encourage you to ask this question when eating out. You will be humbled and surprised in many, many ways!

To positively shape our destiny, we must interact and connect with others on an intimate level. Our intimate, personal relationships with others determines our destiny. Our lives are not meant to be an inward, but an outward journey involving other people, other relationships. When we give to others, in fact, we receive. In other words, we must give away love to keep it.

Many studies suggest that health is affected by our personal connections (or lack thereof). Texting and Facebook are robbing us, and especially our children, of true personal connection with other human beings. Today, one in four Americans does not have anyone they feel close enough with to share a problem. They have "Facebook Friends" but not "Real Friends" - no personal connectivity. It's been determined that the more personally connected we are, the healthier we become. Research shows that personal connectivity, face to face, is directly related to good mental health and physical longevity. In other words, we probably get into bad situations on our own, but we get out of them and begin to heal through personal connectivity with others. I suggest writing a personal, hand written note to a different, close friend every day thanking them for their friendship and participation in your life. I have a stack of personal note cards on my desk to remind me every evening before I leave work. Hand write a personal note to a close acquaintance every day for the rest of your life and watch your connectivity explode and your mental health take a mega-leap! I suggest you make this a high-value activity.

CHAPTER SUMMARY

▲ GOLDEN NUGGETS:

- I'm using the same "road map" to recover from this downfall (addiction) that I used to acquire my original personal, business and financial success.

- I've learned that by surrendering I've joined the winning team.

- It wasn't until I forgave myself that I can forgive others and escape the Bondage of Self.

- Today, one in four Americans do not have anyone they feel close enough with to share a real problem.

- Research shows that personal connectivity, face to face, is directly related to good mental health and physical longevity.

- The process I've described in this book, for building a strategic plan for your life works regardless of personal situation, or personal dilemmas. You don't have to be an addict to benefit from The Mind-Body Crossover and other processes outlined in this book. It works for everyone regardless of your condition.

ACTION ITEMS: (TELL ME WHAT TO DO)

- Grow and expand your connectivity to other people. Set a weekly calendar note to formally ask someone (friend, business associate, co-worker etc.) to coffee, lunch, etc. Every week.

- Set a daily reminder to connect with someone, in person, every day. Be positive and smile more during all these encounters and initiate the contact with a firm, warm handshake and direct eye contact. Come prepared to listen. It's not all about you. Give to the other person by listening to them. Place this important, daily goal on your Buck Card.

- Send a hand-written note to a close friend thanking them for their friendship and participation in your life. Hand write one of these every day for the rest of your life and watch your connectivity explode.

- Hesitation kills!

CHAPTER EIGHTEEN

STEP-BY-STEP

"All hard work brings profit, but mere talk
leads only to poverty."
Proverbs 14:23

Now the work begins! As mentioned at the start of this book, I will provide you a step-by-step process to implement that will change your life. I did not say it would be easy, but it will be fun and change your life if you complete the necessary steps. Here is what I said in the first paragraph of this book:

> "This book is about a proven technique that teaches you how to build a Strategic Plan for Your Life while you grow towards financial security, emotional awareness and eventually spiritual maturity. It's about a Proven Process with a Road Map on how to implement permanent lasting "Change" in your life. No motivational Rah-Rah, only a Process! Implement the Process and it will change your life! Enjoy the ride!"

By now, I hope you realize this process is not a "Get Rich Quick Solution" to solving life's problems. As the adage says, "Nothing worthwhile in life comes without a price." It requires hard work, new habits, a shift in thinking, a tremendous amount of determination, and a lot of humility to secure lasting change. The good news is this process works when fully implemented in a serious manner! Stiffen your resolve, right now, and give the process a fighting chance. Make a determined, mental commitment to excellence and pursue this process with fiery passion. Call on your Higher Power for assistance!

<u>Don't give up until you see the "Miracle" in your life</u>!

HERE WE GO!

ROAD MAP

Below is a chronological listing of things you need to complete to build an inspiring strategic plan for your life. It is a checklist to ensure that you have completed all items assigned in the preceding chapter summaries under ACTION ITEMS, (TELL ME WHAT TO DO). Review these items and start implementing today. Taking action, massive action, is the key to all success.

- Read and take "Strength Finders" personality test by Ross.

- Send out 25-30 emails to friends re your unique ability.

- Take the Birkman Method to surface unique hidden social expectations

- Write your first statement about your personal unique ability.

- Implement the Great I Am exercise.

- Make your List of 500 as outlined.

- Categorize your list into the seven areas of your life.

- Write 7 goal statements for each area of your life - Total 49.

- Create 20-30 personal written mantras.

- Create mantra tapes for meditation.

- Create your personal buck card front and back. Read daily.

- Start a Journal.

- Create a picture board and place it in a visible area.

- Write 7 major goals. One for each area of your life. Review monthly.

- Implement The Countdown process moment by moment

- Implement Rise and Shine daily.

- Create hourly, daily, weekly, monthly, quarterly calendar alarms.

- Join Toastmasters this week.

- Join a service organization. Give back.

- Join your industry association and work to become its President.

- Meditate daily while listening to your mantra and goals audio tape.

- Review your 49 goal statements at the start of every day - Calendar.

- Monitor and rewrite your seven major goals once a month - Calendar.

- Start sending a handwritten card to someone every day

- Start Future Pacing technique when tempted to do something destructive

- Create a notebook - A Strategic Plan for My Life - Include all above items!

"Create a notebook," is probably the most important. It is here where you bring a 100% completion to your quest to obtain all the possibilities discussed in this book. There is no absolute correct way to build this notebook. Use your creativity. The notebook should become your most sacred possession. Keep it nearby and review/rewrite continuously. A high-value activity! Imprinting, triggers and repetition are the keys to my process and your success.

CONCLUSION

In a nutshell, rich, fulfilling lives are lives overflowing with purpose, passion, sacrifice, humility, service and maturity. There is no free ticket, no get rich quick scheme in this world that works. We must take 100% responsibility for what happens to us if we want to experience an abundance filled journey. Once we stop blaming others and accept 100% responsibility, we can give up our self-pity, victimization, passive aggressive behavior and resentments. Then we can start our ongoing quest for spiritual maturity leading us to a life filled with pure joy! Today, God has placed eternity in my heart. It starts with an "intellectual hunger" to search, grow and mature. Living a life of moderation instead of MORE.

We each need to enlarge our spiritual connection by enlarging connectivity to others. Insisting on, always being "right", being a martyr, and being a victim is tiresome, very tiresome, and a huge waste of time! People suffering from victimization are fear based and don't like to consider new thoughts that take them out of their comfort zone. They fight establishing new habits because of fear. Get rid of your victimization. Blaming others is a massive maturity shortfall. It results in us being victims of a war we are waging against ourselves!

We must learn to address this problem by forming new healthier habits. We must realize that everyone else is focused on their issues, not ours. We must take 100% responsibility for ourselves, because no one else will! It starts with self-examination, then self-forgiveness and then new habit formation. Holding anger towards others and ourselves is poisonous. It poisons our outlook on the world and our universe. We must learn to forgive across the board because we all have hurt others along our own personal journey. We must accept responsibility for shortfalls and admit character defects, if we want to grow, heal and reach maturity. Living a double life, an outside life and an inside life is no longer acceptable to me. My old "false self" is slowly being dissolved: self-will run riot, self-delusion, bondage of self and an out of control ego are being replaced with surrender to a higher power! Thank God!

The system outlined in this book can effect a transformative change in your life if taken seriously with an appropriate amount of denial and discipline. Future Pacing, The Countdown, The Mind-Body Crossover, triggers, imprinting, creative visualization, meditation, repetition, assessment testing and prayer are secrets and tools necessary to create a "Strategic Plan for Your Life" that will transform your existence into a life filled with pure, exhilarating joy! Remember that hesitation kills!

The steps are fully outlined, but it is up to you to develop the "details" and build "A Strategic Plan for Your Life". Be alerted to the "Complacency Trap" in your quest for greatness. William Pollard once warned "The arrogance of success is to think that what you did yesterday will be sufficient for tomorrow". We all become complacent and fall short from time to time. Be diligently, aware and reboot when necessary. As your last assignment, you set a calendar tickler to reread the chapter summaries of this book at the beginning of every month to help stay enthused and on track. Repetition is the key to all achievement!

After my downfall of addiction and financial collapse, I could finally see the benefit of every past mistake, misread and wrong turn. I finally realized that instead of regretting my past, I must become friends with it, if truly wanting to grow and mature. I knew that being a mentor and speaker was the most powerful way to experience a tremendous amount of pure joy. Today, I am focused on using my unique ability to make a difference in the lives of others, by helping others. I firmly believe the nature of humanity is to stand up for one another. We all need connection to other people to successfully fulfill our Destiny!

"WHEN THE STUDENT'S READY, THE TEACHER WILL APPEAR!"

Every New Year's Day I send out the following message to many of my close personal friends:

Happy New Year!

"Your destiny is shaped by the quality of your personal relationships!"

In Addition to You!

I Also Choose a Personal Relationship With

JESUS CHRIST!

THE END

EXHIBIT A

A good friend who witnessed my growth over the last few years sent me this message via his blog. It has been a special message considering my battle with alcohol and experiences with "Whiskey River" and the author of the song in this blog. The blog is written by a dear friend Robert McBurnett who knew about some of my life story from talks I had given at spiritual retreats that he and I attended together. He substituted my name with "Glen" as he wrote the blog and could not get in touch with me about using my real name in the blog from an anonymity perspective. I was touched by his comments below even though I did not know Willie as well as expressed in this blog, as he was only a general one-time acquaintance:

To: "Gary F. Dahse" <garydahse@gmail.com>
From: Robert McBurnett

> The theme of this blog is "Exploring life as it unfolds in the context of scripture; finding meaning by heightening awareness of God in the day to day". This musing is a testament to seeing God where you might least expect him in the day to day. I love how God can speak to us using something so very far removed from where he is and what he wants for us.
>
> Whiskey River take my mind.
> Don't let her memory torture me.
> Whiskey River don't run dry,
> You're all I've got take care of me.
>
> I'm drowning in a whiskey river,

Bathing my mem'ried mind in the wetness of its soul.
Feeling the amber current flowing from my mind,
And warm an empty heart you left so cold.

Whiskey River take my mind.
Don't let her memory torture me.
Whiskey River don't run dry,
You're all I've got take care of me. -Willie Nelson

If you're of a certain age (and I most assuredly am), you know the song, as well as the artist and it is now raging in your head.

This song is a lament – not a bluesy lament – a rip-roaring, shot out of a cannon lament. Willie Nelson starts virtually every concert with this song for that very reason. It immediately gets the crowd engaged, on their feet and dialed into the music. Not only that, some of Willie's very best guitar work is on display in Willie Nelson's unmistakable style.

It is a song about the pain of lost love, of a lost relationship. It is about recovery. It is about romance. Aside from the amazing artistry Willie brought to it, the attraction is that, so many have suffered the extreme pain of being left behind by their "one true love" connecting them intimately with the pain and temptation of his source of relief expressed in this song.

I wish I could tell you I was drawn to the song for those reasons, but alas I was not. I gravitated to the song because I aspired to have such a relationship and to have known the intense love that would precede such pain, but that is a story for another day (maybe).

I could also tell you that I was recently driving along, and the song came on the radio, but I won't. I could tell you that I was listening to my iPod on shuffle and it came up (which it could because it is indeed on the iPod), but I won't. In truth, I was just hustling along the path of an otherwise ordinary day, tending to business, and it popped in my head. Without motive or thought in mind, I stopped and listened to it play in my head hearing the words as well as the music, when I heard another voice singing an alternate lyric.

Holy Spirit take my mind.
Don't let my memories torture me.
Holy Spirit don't run dry,
You're all I've got take care of me.

I'm drowning in the Holy Spirit,
Bathing my mem'ried mind in the fullness of its soul.
Feeling the Spirit's current flowing through my mind,
And warm an empty heart the world left so cold.

Holy Spirit take my mind.
Don't let my memories torture me.
Holy Spirit don't run dry,
You're all I've got take care of me.

Let's be clear – I am not suggesting we will be singing this in worship anytime soon, but it sent many messages of assurance my way. For a start, the world constantly leaves me cold and empties my heart. And having tried many means of finding relief and recovery from what the world sends my way, I have learned the one that works is the Holy Spirit. I feel its current flowing in to flood my mind; it is as mentally soothing as a warm bath. In the final analysis, it truly is all I've got, and I am indeed counting on it to take care of me.

As much as this song reminds me of who I was and who I might have become, (and maybe it does for some of you as well) it also reminds me of role models and their paths through life. I am specifically indebted to a friend – let's call him Glen. Glen is a great role model for me. STRONG in the faith, just far enough ahead of me on the path to Christ that I can learn from his example, but not so far ahead that I can't stay within shouting distance. His eyes are truly fixed on Jesus and it resonates in everything he does. His compassion for others knows no bounds. He is never so busy that he doesn't stop, sit and listen when someone is hurting – sometimes even when nothing is said, he just senses someone's pain or need. I don't ever recall a time where his response to any call was, "Well, you know in 4th Kings, the 82nd chapter . . .." His response is a tender, "Tell me more about it". I seem to remember a long-ago carpenter who responded similarly to all who came his way.

I had known Glen for some time, admired his character, aspired to follow his lead and felt I knew him well. Then one day, he gave another part of his life story I hadn't heard. Early in life, Glen was a confederate of Willie – yes, the Willie

Nelson. Rode the busses, played golf and I don't want to know what all else, but I'm sure it included "all else." When Waylon Jennings sang, "Let's go to Luckenbach, Texas with Willie and Waylon and the boys," Glen was one of those boys I am quite sure.

Glen now bathes in the fullness of the Holy Spirit. It warms his heart and floods his mind. It truly is all he has . . . and it takes care of him. And Glen leads me down the path to a closer and closer relationship with Christ.

Thank you, Glen. Thank you, Willie. Thank you, Holy Spirit.

Come Holy Spirit, you're all I've got take care of me!

ABOUT THE AUTHOR

LIFE PLAN - WHO I AM

I "BE" long to God. I am His child, and that practiced, disciplined awareness has stilled my monkey-mind. He is washing me clean and speaking with me constantly, and I remember when I look in His eyes, and He shows up constantly, including in my eyes. I am alive with His Life, totally by grace, and I can laugh at myself, because I love myself, secure in His Love for me. Caring, empathetic, sensitive and comfortable in my skin, I have no need to possess another's skin or emotions to feel better, and I have no concern for what others think about me or the integrity journey I'm on, now in full possession of my fear, no longer ruled by it. Slender and fit, awake and alive, loving fine foods, fragrance and fellowship, I walk through life with healthfulness and vitality. In my partnership with a woman, I am emotionally aware and spiritually mature, with love flowing naturally without effort, expectation, or obligation. We are freely giving, a perfect fit, anticipating each other's steps in a graceful dance, caring, excited, intimate, and passionate. We are eager and willing to talk tirelessly about meaningful things, and out of that closeness our sexuality flows powerfully, illuminated by God's Love. We connect based on what's real, not on shallow surface appeal, with wisdom flowing from God, not our efforts at successful performance. I am an available and deeply connected Dad - focused and attentive, clean and sober - and my kids feel my devotion and the power of my recovery. Matt is my successful dynamo, a natural entrepreneur, and I give him the gift of God's wisdom and grace flowing through me. Morgan is my intense Pitbull, clear and focused on excellence and willing, and I give her the gift of intimate connection and total presence. I honor the pain of divorce that Carol and I have put them through and stand for my kids knowing that they are loved and blessed by both of their parents. I appreciate the pain & struggle of my parents' lives, and how it formed the soil of the thriving tree that is my life today, with Matt & Morgan as the fruit. My Dad's warm, yet broken and crushed spirit and my Mom's intelligence and creativity fed my soul and challenged me to grow, learn and transcend. I live as my deepest hug and thank you tribute for the incredible resolve of Fred & Christine. I am so glad I will re-join them someday in heaven. I appreciate my sister, Susan, more than words can say; I will always drop everything and run to her if she needs me. We share mutual generosity, support & love, unconditionally, and I give her the gift of our equality, mutual respect, & heart of Jesus as a true friend, I am living generosity as the thankful prodigal; I have needed grace, so I have it to pour into my friends' lives. I am the hope of God incarnate, bringing my friends the maturity and wisdom that can only come from hitting bottom and letting go. A natural mentor amid community, people gravitate to me naturally, where they fall in love with themselves for the first time. I help people give up their victimhood, discovering their ability to access joy and passion through their unique giftedness. My calling is so much fun that I almost feel guilty, but not quite. I do work and help others in a way that makes me cry. A brave beacon of a man, while fully human, lit up to share that the man I've always judged - me - is beautiful, as is. I travel the world speaking to the wealthy and spoiled, helping shift consciousness from fear and greed to the love of God. I help organizations transform through spoken and written word, bringing my own death and resurrection into service, allowing God to have me completely.

Life Plan Co-Authors:

Jim Spivey

Gary Dahse

P.S. I highly recommend you consider Jim Spivey if you are considering a Life Plan. His goal is that every person in the world, eventually has a written Life Plan!

Jim can be reached at:
jim.spivey@Mazzipartners.com www.mazzipartners.com.

BIOGRAPHY

Gary F. Dahse

Career Summary

Gary F. Dahse has 35 years' experience in consulting and motivational training. He is the author of Tell Me What To Do, a self-help book focused on how to build a strategic plan for your life. Recognized internationally as a motivational Keynote Speaker and instructor in the field of organizational behavior, his focus is helping high powered corporations mitigate consternation in the "C-Suite". Mr. Dahse also consults with corporations and highly successful entrepreneurs teaching them how to develop their unique attributes and abilities. His seminars are strategically designed to help these entities recognize their full potential. He travels extensively and works with individuals and corporate entities globally.

Education

Mr. Dahse holds a BA from Our Lady of the Lake University and attended Texas Lutheran College and the University of Texas at Austin majoring in Business Administration.

Professional Affiliations

Mr. Dahse is licensed by the Texas Real Estate Commission as a broker and Realtor. In addition to his consulting business, he has been involved in the commercial real estate business for 40 years. He previously acted as a principal and owner of Rubloff, Inc., one of the largest privately held commercial real estate firms in the country. Having successfully recruited over 145 brokers in numerous markets in the Southwest, Mr. Dahse is also recognized as a high-performance sales trainer. He is a past president of the Institute of Real Estate Management and former member of the board of directors of the Building Owners and Managers Association – Houston Chapter.

Community Service

Mr. Dahse is active in community affairs. He previously worked in a prison ministry, Bridges to Life, which focuses on bringing prisoners together with their victims to help facilitate the healing process. He is a Past President of the Board of Directors for the ESCAPE Center for Abused Children, served as a Division Director for the Texas Gulf Coast District of Exchange, and as President of the Exchange Club of the Magic Circle.

You can contact Gary at:

www.garydahse.com

garydahse@gmail.com

Made in the USA
Lexington, KY
11 May 2019